For *all* examination candidates an essential ingredient for success is one which is rarely taught, little appreciated and not properly understood — no matter how well taught or learned the subject matter is. That ingredient is *Exam Technique*. It applies equally to any exam, whatever the subject matter, level, or language. Few possess it naturally; most must develop it for themselves.

This book is written for *all* students taking examinations whether at secondary, further or higher education levels. The book itself is not limited to any one 'level'. The principles of successful exam technique apply to a wide range of students, including those attending nightschool or day release classes, art or technical colleges or other centres of higher education. It includes full- and part-time students, or those studying in community centres or at home, and mature students who may not have taken an exam for years. And it includes those returning to education in later life, who may never have sat an examination before at all.

Successful exam technique can be learned and applied by everyone. With just a little effort it will bring you much improved results, and enable you to face *your* examination with the confidence of one who is fully prepared.

Successful
EXAM
Technique

David Cocker

Northcote House

British Library Cataloguing in Publication Data

Cocker, David
    Successful exam technique.
    1. Examinations — Great Britain — Study guides
    I. Title
    371.3′028′12   LB3060.57

    ISBN 0-7463-0348-3

First published in 1987 by Northcote House Publishers Ltd,
Harper & Row House, Estover Road, Plymouth PL6 7PZ,
United Kingdom. Tel: Plymouth (0752) 705251. Telex: 45635.

Printed and bound in Great Britain by
A. Wheaton & Co. Ltd., Exeter

Contents

Introduction

Anyone with common sense can pass exams. Doing well in examinations is not difficult, and passing should be easy with just a bit of effort. Exams are easy to pass — they have to be. In fact, they are usually designed so that most students will pass. It is no use designing an exam so that most students will fail! Of course *some* students will fail examinations, because it is equally no use if *all* students pass an examination. With proper preparation and technique you can ensure that *you* are not one of those who fails.

Success depends on you

Success depends on you, and you alone. Others can and will help, of course — parents, teachers, instructors and tutors — but it is up to you to *seek* that help. Remember, there is nothing silly about studying hard and doing well in examinations, nor is there anything clever about failing or being unemployed. Don't worry about what your friends may say or think. They will have plenty of time to regret their mistakes. The *fact* is that exams are the key to success and a good job and career.

Common sense

This book does not contain any magic formulas for passing examinations; it is essentially based on common sense. Unfortunately this is what is most lacking. So many students rush into exams not knowing what to expect, or how to cope, believing that all they have to do is write as much as possible in the time allowed.

This book is about bringing a systematic ordered approach to the examination from the earliest days of your course, right through study and revision, to the examination itself. The book will help you develop a **highly-ordered**, **intensive** system of revision and study, along with a **time-efficient** approach to your examination which is designed to maximise marks and improve your final result. The book explains the whole examination system, to help you get the best from it; it looks at the things which can, and often do, go wrong, in order to eliminate them.

Taking exams can sometimes seem like gambling on a horse race. But there is one big difference — *you are in a position to manipulate the odds in your favour*. The gambling element arises as to what questions come up, what topics you have studied, and so can answer questions on. But the better prepared you are in understanding the exact form and nature of the examination facing you, as well as having systematically covered the topics in your subject, then the more the odds are in your favour. The better will be your chance of success — not only in passing, but in doing really well. Good technique is the key to help you achieve this.

Why Exams?

There has been growing criticism in recent years of examinations as a means of assessing students. However, it must be said that so far no-one has come up with a much better alternative. The only real alternative — **continuous assessment** — is itself open to criticism. In one form, it amounts to a series of tests or mini-exams over a period of time. If these are removed completely, assessment becomes the subjective view of one person (the instructor). It is open to problems of favouritism or personality clashes — even instructors are only human. And work done by students out of class, away from the watchful eye of the instructor, may not be their own unaided work.

Critics will say examinations are nothing more than a test of memory, legibility of handwriting, or the ability to work under stress. But surely these are desirable qualities? If a student uses his or her qualification to get a job, a good memory is usually an asset in doing that job. It is no use if the employee has to keep rushing off to look up things he or she cannot remember. Legible handwriting, too, is not only an asset but a necessity in modern society (unless we are going to walk around with typewriters under our arms). We have to write letters, notes, memos or reports, or fill in forms of various kinds throughout our lives. And prospective employers are not likely to give a job to someone whose application form they cannot decipher! In any case, examination markers are not looking for works of art; they simply want to read what the student has written. Usually where a word is mis-spelt or hard to read, the marker will give the candidate the benefit of the doubt if he possibly can.

An ability to work under stress is important, too. It is not enough to be good at a subject; the student may progress to a responsible job with pressure or stress in some form and will have to cope with this to be successful.

The best form of assessment may be some combination of continuous assessment and exams. But this is a highly debatable topic, beyond the scope of this handbook. The fact is that most students are stuck with the examination system, and we must deal with it and make the best of it, which is the purpose of this book.

Exams — basic purposes

The function of an examination is not to terrorise students, nor to show how stupid or how bright one is. It is to show that a student has studied a subject to a certain level, in a certain depth, for a certain period of time, and has reached a certain standard of understanding. The people who need such proof may be prospective employers who need to know that the student has the knowledge to carry out the job on offer; or they may be those in higher education who need to know that the student has reached a certain standard before going on to a more advanced course which takes for granted information learned earlier.

It is a fact of life that some people are better at one thing than another. The examination system helps to sort out these differences, to produce an ordered society where each of us can find the best place for our particular skills and abilities. It is for the students to choose their subjects to match their skills and abilities, and then to maximise their results to do the best for themselves. No matter how far they may progress, they will at least know they have done their best, and have found the best place in society for them.

Your opportunity

Look on your examination as an opportunity to show other people what you can do. There is no shame in failure, if you have really tried your best. Try harder next time, or try something else which you feel you can do better. Never give up learning or trying to improve your chances. It is your *right* — don't throw it away!

Will Exams Help *You*?

- ☐ Qualify for a place in further or higher education?
- ☐ Get onto an important training scheme?
- ☐ Prove your abilities to an employer?
- ☐ Help you build your chosen career?
- ☐ Help you earn more money?
- ☐ Help you get a better and more interesting job?
- ☐ Help you make up for past mistakes?
- ☐ Give you a second chance in life?
- ☐ Help you compete successfully with others?
- ☐ Help you win promotion?
- ☐ Help to get you further grants?

It really is easy to pass exams if you know at least something about the subject you have been studying for the last year or two. If you don't know this minimum then you shouldn't yet be taking that subject.

Example

An example will serve to illustrate this point. Let's consider an examination where six questions have to be answered from a choice of eight. Let's assume the questions will each be marked out of 20 and the pass mark will be 40% (8 marks per question or 48 marks total). A poor student looks at the question page, and out of his *whole* one or two years' study can see only *one* question out of the whole eight that he can do. He does this reasonably well, but misses out several points in his first answer.

RESULT: Question 1 — 15 marks out of 20

Not bad, but the student is in trouble already and struggling to find another question; at least another 33 marks are needed for a pass.

For the second question, a definition is required (which the student can't remember); the rest is in two parts, only one of which the student knows something about and does reasonably well on. Some attempt at the second part gains a couple of marks.

RESULT: Question 6 definition — 0 marks out of 2
Question 6 (a) — 7 marks out of 9
Question 6 (b) — 2 marks out of 9
Total — 9 marks out of 20

The third question tackled is a multiple choice question, a quick and easy source of marks:

Question 3. Answer 8 from the following 12 (2½ marks each).

This student only knows 2 of the facts from the 12 asked and gets them right. A third answer is correctly guessed and gets the marks; and a further attempt is only half right. Two answers are wrong and the rest (half the question) is not even attempted.

RESULT: 3 x 2½ marks, plus 1¼ marks = 8¾ marks. Total 9/20.

With panic subsiding somewhat — the candidate feeling there is plenty of time to think — he spots something he knows in half of one question and gets some of it right. But he hasn't a clue about the rest of the question and makes no attempt at it.

RESULT: Question 2 — 1st half 6/10, 2nd half 0/10. Total 6/20.

The student has two more questions to find and struggling in the depths of his brain finds something he feels he can handle. The question is in three parts — a calculation, a description of a process, and an explanation of an event. The calculation is wrong but the formula is right and the brief working shows it was tackled in the right way. The description of a process is rubbish but the right diagram is drawn; the explanation of the event shows fudged principles but some inkling of an idea.

RESULT: Question 4 — calculation 2/7 (for method), description 2/7 (for diagram), explanation 3/6 (half right). Total 7/20.

At this stage the student has exhausted his knowledge except for Question 8 which he knows nothing about, apart from the definition. He makes no attempt at the rest of the question.

RESULT: Question 8 — definition 2/2, rest 0/18. Total 2/20.

This student clearly knows very little and is surely a hopeless case. Surely he has failed this subject which he has studied and prepared for for one/ two years? **But let's examine the marks:**

	Marks	*Total*	
Question 1	15	20	
Question 6	9	20	
Question 3	9	20	
Question 2	6	20	
Question 4	7	20	
Question 8	2	20	
Total	48	120	= 40% (a pass!)

This student has passed! It just shows *how bad* you have to be to fail. Notice in Question 8 how vital the two marks turned out to be for this pass. If the last question had not been attempted at all, the student would have *failed!*

Main Examining Boards

GCE Boards

Associated Examining Board (AEB)
Wellington House
Station Road
Aldershot
Hants GU11 1BQ
Tel: (0252) 25551

Cambridge University Local
Examinations Syndicate
Syndicate Buildings
17 Harvey Road
Cambridge CB1 2EU
Tel: (0223) 61111

Joint Matriculation Board (JMB)
Manchester M15 6EU
Tel: (061) 273 2565
Syllabuses and Regulations from:
J Sherratt & Sons, Publishers
Park Road, Timperley, Cheshire.

Northern Ireland Schools
Examinations Council
Beechill House
42 Beechill Road
Belfast BT8 4RS
Tel: (Belfast) 704666

Oxford & Cambridge Schools
Examination Board
Elsfield Way
Oxford OX2 8EP
Tel: (0865) 54421 or
Brook House
10 Trumpington Street
Cambridge CB2 1QB
Tel: (0223) 64326

Oxford Delegacy of Local
Examinations
Ewart Place
Summertown
Oxford OX2 7BZ
Tel: (0865) 54291

Southern Universities Joint
Board for School Examinations
Cotham Road
Bristol
Avon BS6 6DD
Tel: (0272) 561231

University of London School
Examinations Council
66-72 Gower Street
London WC1E 6EE
Tel: (01) 636 8000
Publications Department:
50 Gordon Square, London WC1H 0PJ.

Welsh Joint Education Committe
245 Western Avenue
Cardiff CF5 2YX
Tel: (0222) 561231

GCSE Boards

For the purpose of GCSE the GCE and CSE Boards have come together in regional groups and further information is available from any of the individual Boards listed above.

Further education

Business & Technician Education
Council (BTEC)
Central House
Upper Woburn Place
London WC1H 0HH
Tel: (01) 388 3288

City & Guilds of London Institute
76 Portland Place
London W1N 4AA
Tel: (01) 580 3050

London Chamber of Commerce
& Industry Examinations Board (LCCI)
Marlowe House
Station Road
Sidcup
Kent DA15 7BJ
Tel: (01) 302 0261-4

Pitman Examinations Institute
Catteshall Manor
Godalming
Surrey GU7 1UU
Tel: (04868) 5311

Royal Society of Arts
Examinations Board (RSA)
John Adam Street
Adelphi
London WC2N 6EZ
Tel: (01) 839 2366

Further information

A comprehensive listing of courses and qualifications can be found in the annual publication *British Qualifications* available in most reference libraries, published by Kogan Page (London).

Read the Rules and Regulations

All public examinations are held according to various rules and regulations. The authority which sets the examination will publish these in the form of a leaflet or notice — *Rules and Regulations*. Try to read a copy of these, preferably before starting your study/revision leading up to the examination. If you have to register for the examination yourself, you will normally be sent a copy with the application forms. But in most cases, where groups of students are entered by a school, college or other institution, copies will be posted on notice boards, or be available from the secretary's office or from instructors. In cases of difficulty you could write off for your own copy.

The rules and regulations set out exactly how the examinations are to be run, what is allowed, and what is not. They will cover all such things as dates for publication of results and appeals procedures. You need not own your own copy but you should have at least read and understood what it contains so that you understand the main rules and regulations, and know where to get further information if necessary.

Model Letter

To: The Secretary
XYZ Examinations Board   Date

Dear Sir

Student rules and regulations

I write to ask whether you could please send me a copy of the current rules and regulations relating to candidates preparing for the examination in (name of examination). I am a student and hope to enter for this examination.

If you make a small charge for this publication I should be glad to pay the same immediately upon receipt of your invoice.

Yours faithfully

Name

A syllabus for a course — whether for a week or a couple of years — sets out the major topics and areas of study of that course. The course is so designed that all the material in the syllabus can be covered in the time allotted for study, with extramural work where appropriate.

The syllabus will not only tell you what may be examined, it will also tell you what will *not*. If a topic is not on the syllabus, it simply will not be examined. But remember, a syllabus is only a general outline, a skeleton of topics to be fleshed out by the instructor or student. Thus the student should, as far as possible, have studied all the topics on the syllabus before taking the exam.

- Get your own copy of the syllabus.
- Refer to it from time to time as the course proceeds.
- Mark off topics as you or your class have dealt with them.
- Towards the end of the course, before serious revision, try to identify and fill any gaps. Discuss these with your instructor, and do some home study if you can.

In class examinations, only those topics you have studied recently are examined, but in public examinations the *whole range* of the syllabus may be examined. The examiners will not be concerned that you have only studied so and so, or have not had time to do this or that.

Topics not covered in teaching

It can sometimes happen that, for one reason or another, some topics are not covered by the instructor, and have to be left out. This may be for lack of money, equipment or even knowledge (not even the best teachers know everything). There could be other special reasons; for example, it would be hard to explore the ecology of a shore line environment if one lived and studied several hundred miles from the sea; theory may be only of limited value here. However, when setting the syllabus the examiners do make allowances, and in the latter case may state that one or two local environments can be studied on a practical basis allowing for study of the seashore, if close, or else the local fields or woods or even inner city urban environment. The questions on such a topic will always be worded so as to let all students answer on the basis of their own experience or study.

Arrangement of topics and questions

It may be, however, that certain students will not have been able to study certain topics and this is usually allowed for in public examinations by offering *more* questions on the examination paper than have to be answered. For example, *Answer 6 questions from 8* or *Answer Questions 1 and any other 3 (from 5)*. In the latter case Question 1 is compulsory; it *must* be answered by all candidates, regardless of what parts of the syllabus they may or may not have studied. This is usually because the topic is fundamental to the whole subject; it is normally indicated on the syllabus, made clear by the instructor, or evident from a study of past papers. For example, one of the papers leading to the Mastership of Chemical Analysis offered by the Royal Society of Chemistry *always* has a compulsory question dealing with the filling in and completion of public analysts' report forms; it carries 60% of the marks on that paper. This is because the qualification (M.Chem.A.) is the basic one for Public Analysts and so this ability is vital and has to be fully tested.

Subjects and Topics

Examples of main subjects and their topics

SUBJECT	MAIN TOPICS	TOPICS	SUB TOPICS	AREAS
BIOLOGY	Botany (Plants)	Flowering	Roots	Types, Function, Structure
			Stem	Function, Structure
			Leaves	Types, Function, Structure
		non-Flowering		
	Ecology	Practical		Fields, Woods, Streams
		Theoretical		
HISTORY	Ancient	Primitive, Greek, Roman		
	Medieval	Social, Ecclesiastical, Military		
	Modern	British	Social, Political, Economic	
		European	Hapsburg, Bourbon, Ottoman	
		American	Pre-Civil War, Post-Civil War	

In this section, and elsewhere, the word **subject** will be used to mean the whole of a course leading to an examination in that subject. This may include several main **topics** of study which then divide into various sub-topics or points of study. You can benefit from recognising this structure, for example as shown on the opposite page.

In schools *each subject* is normally taught by a single teacher, for example Geography or Maths. But in college and elsewhere individual topics *within* a main subject will probably be dealt with by one or more separate instructors, each specialising in their own field. Each topic in the course will probably contain several areas of study; a topic is usually the amount of material that could form the basis of a question in the examination paper. Main topics may produce several questions, or even separate sections of questions. The areas of study within a topic may form the basis of a question separately (i.e. any particular question on a topic may be drawn only from a small area of the whole topic), or in some combination (i.e. a series of parts in a question may examine various areas of the topic).

Example

Let us take the case of a question paper with six questions on a subject of three main topics. Normally, two questions would be on each topic (possibly in separate sections). In the case of a subject with six topics and eight questions on the paper, each topic will have a question and the other two questions will probably be drawn from the more important topics. A choice may (or may not) be given, so it may (or may not) be possible to avoid weaker areas.

With a subject of eight topics and six questions, two topics may not be examined at all, but you should prepare for *all* topics since you will not be able to tell which two will be left out. Alternatively the smaller topics may be given half questions, and two smaller topics combined to make one question of two parts.

Preparation for the exam should start at the very beginning of your course. This is the way to get the best results. Don't leave it until a few weeks before the exam, when it will probably be too late to make much difference.

Taking notes

It is vitally important throughout your course to take **proper notes** from lectures or classes or, if you are studying at home, to make your own notes. Don't just sit there in class listening to the instructor and think you will be able to remember the information in a year's time — you simply won't! Use the time to write up a set of notes before you forget important points. A proper set of notes is one of the keys to examination success. It will serve as the core of your revision work later on.

Making your own notes

It is important, too, that they should be your *own* notes, and not those of someone else. Everyone makes notes in different ways. Also you can read your own handwriting best; you don't want to be struggling to decipher somone else's handwriting during your revision. Notes are just that, not a word-for-word copy of what has been said in class. Certain things during note-making may have been left out as understood. Only the person making the notes, therefore, can really make proper use of them.

Technique of taking notes

Notes are best made on loose sheets of paper, A4, foolscap or quarto sizes normally available in pads. Keep them in a folder of some kind, rather than writing in 'bound' notebooks. This will make it easier to add notes, or change them around as you go along.

Taking good notes is a **skill** which needs to be developed and mastered in a manner which suits you. No two people's methods will be the same. It is impossible to get down everything the instructor may say during the class unless you do shorthand/dictation. In fact, it is usually unnecessary to do so. What you really need is the essence of the topic, in other words enough detail to let you read your notes later on and recall the ideas and facts your instructor was discussing, and understand them as well as you did when it was given. Don't try to write down long sentences, you will fall behind and get lost. Write down part-sentences, phrases or just key words.

Shorthand ideas

Develop your own private shorthand to write things down in a faster and shorter form.

For example, you can use **acronyms** — words made up from the initial letters of a phrase or series of words:

> WHO — **W**orld **H**ealth **O**rganisation
> NATO — **N**orth **A**tlantic **T**reaty **O**rganisation
> ACTH — **A**dreno **C**orticotropic **H**ormone
> LFER — **L**inear **F**ree **E**nergy **R**elationship

Use capital letters for these words to avoid confusion.

You can also **abbreviate** long words in some way. Many words have the same endings which can be abbreviated, for example:

-meter	$\rightarrow$	-m-	thermometer	$\rightarrow$	thermom-
			altimeter	$\rightarrow$	altim-
-ism	$\rightarrow$	$^{-m}$	symbolism	$\rightarrow$	$symbol^{m}$
			dichroism	$\rightarrow$	$dichro^{m}$
-sion	$\rightarrow$	$^{-n}$	tension	$\rightarrow$	$tens^{n}$
-tion	$\rightarrow$	$^{-n}$	solution	$\rightarrow$	$solut^{n}$
-ment	$\rightarrow$	$^{-t}$	assessment	$\rightarrow$	$assess^{t}$
			contentment	$\rightarrow$	$content^{t}$
-ent	$\rightarrow$	$^{-t}$	solvent	$\rightarrow$	$solv^{t}$

You'll find it much quicker to write one letter than three or four. With words which crop up regularly in your subject you will soon become familiar with this system.

Again you can use **half words**, especially if they are words that occur often:

> Ans. — Answer
> Res. — Result
> Ref. — Reference, in reference to
> Sep. — Separate
> Coef. — Coefficient

Abbreviations

Use a variety of **symbols** to indicate movement or relationships, for example:

+)	
&)	Plus, and, as well as, etc
♉)	
x	multiply, times etc
∴	therefore
→	go to, leads to, becomes, transforms into etc
⟶↗	increasing
⟶↘	decreasing
›	greater than
‹	less than
»	much greater than
↑	upper limit, rises to, increases
↓	lower limit, falls to, decreases
=	equal to
≠	not equal to, is different from

Use **numbers** rather than words wherever you can:

17	seventeen
340,000)	
340k)	three hundred and forty thousand
340t)	
10^{-1}	one tenth
$\frac{1}{10}$	one tenth

Use the **symbolism of the subject** where appropriate. For example, in chemistry use **chemical formulae**:

H_2O	Water
$NaCl$	Sodium chloride, common salt
H_2SO_4	Sulphuric acid

Use **single letters** for common words, either alone or mixed with symbols:

N	North
S	South
S.ly	Southerly
S↓)	
S.wards)	Southwards
w̄	with
w̄out	without
ŵ	where
ŵas	whereas

Use a brief **sketch** or **diagram** instead of word or phrase, if it is quicker, or to convey a whole series of ideas or information. For example:

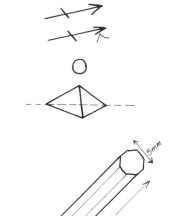

dipole, vector

dipolar

circle, round, circular, spherical.

triangular pyramidal

A brass body or rod 1 meter long having an octagonal cross section and eight flat faces along its length with a uniform thickness (apex to apex) of five millimeters

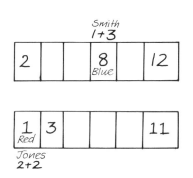

In the street under study — Park Rd., there are two rows of six each, terraced houses. In number one which is painted red lives the Jones family of two adults and two children. Across the road lower down in number eight which is painted blue, are their friends, the Smith family, of one adult and three children . . .

Your own system

Your abbreviations will depend on yourself and your own thought processes, as well as the subject involved. Slightly different short-hand may be better for different subjects. It may seem hard at first, but you will soon become used to your abbreviations with practice. Whatever you use, it is vital that you can read and understand them easily, without confusion, later on. If in doubt then write them out more fully. As you become familiar with your abbreviations and symbols, add new ones as you go along.

Try to **understand the material** the instructor is discussing in class while making your notes. If you don't understand it then write it down as best you can and think about it afterwards. **Discuss** it with your classmates and/or your instructor until you *do* understand it really clearly. **Adjust your notes** to make quite sure you'll still be able to understand it later on. Use **arrows and notes** freely in the **margins** to tie together ideas, or show how things may be related to one another.

Diagrams
Use plenty of **diagrams**. A clearly drawn well-labelled diagram is worth hundreds of words and is much quicker to do.

Handouts
Instructors will sometimes issue 'handouts' which may be a sheet or whole set of notes. This will save you a lot of writing but don't take *no* further notes at all and rely on the handout alone. It may not be in a form which suits your style of note-taking, or it may not make things fully clear to you. Use the handout as a *basis* for your own notes, adding more information or clarification as the lecture proceeds. You may be able to do this on the handout itself or on a separate piece of paper.

References
Where references are given for **further reading**, note them down and leave a couple of blank lines in your notes. When you come to look up the reference make a few short notes in the space left; indicate what it deals with, and its possible value to you. Then, when you come to revise you will know whether it is worth using in more detail.

A reference may be given with the intention that you should **cover the material for yourself**; in other words the material is on the syllabus but will not be covered in class. In this case, look up the reference, read it through, and make sure you thoroughly understand it. Make a set of notes as if the material had been given to you in class, and put them into the correct place in your class notes.

Reviewing your notes
After each class, or at the end of the day, **go through your notes**. Make sure

- you understand the material and
- are satisfied with your notes.

Adjust and add to them where necessary. This can seem rather tedious, but it doesn't take long and is well worth doing. It will be too late if you come to revision and find your notes unsatisfactory.

Missed classes or lectures

If you miss out on any classes or sessions through illness or some other cause, make sure you catch up on that material. **Borrow** another student's notes. **Discuss** with him/her what was covered and if necessary consult your instructor. Then **write up** your *own* set of notes on the material (don't just photocopy someone else's) and make sure you thoroughly **understand** it.

The syllabus

Throughout your course, look at the syllabus from time to time. Towards the end of the course fill in any major gaps by studying that topic yourself. You may have to do this earlier if the instructor tells you that he/she will not be covering a topic due to lack of time. However, you won't have to study anything on the syllabus that your instructor tells you not to; the syllabus itself may be undergoing change or that topic may not be examined for some reason. If in doubt seek the advice of your instructor.

Textbooks can seem very expensive today. Indeed, they always have been expensive in relation to a student's resources. Great care should be taken, therefore, when deciding what to buy. It would be a complete waste of money to buy *every* book mentioned on a course, though one or more key books may well be essential.

Advance/preliminary reading

Textbooks and other study material fall into several broad categories. Firstly, before starting a course students may be given an **advance reading list**. This may mention books or articles in journals or magazines. It is usually unnecessary to buy any of this material unless the book concerned is the **core text**.

However, you should try to familiarise yourself with as much of this material as you can. It is intended to ensure that all new students, wherever they come from, will be familiar with the same material before they start. It may be that this material won't be covered in the course, and that it will be taken for granted that all students are familiar with it. If you have not gone through it you may find difficulty in coping with the course. On the other hand the material may be treated in greater detail during the course itself, and having gone over it yourself you will find it easier to follow. It will also make your note-taking easier.

This material may not directly form part of the course but rather may be extra reading for those students who wish to broaden their view of the subject, beyond what the course will provide. In this case concentrate your efforts first of all on the material directly relevant to the course. Only read the other material if you want to, if you have time, or if it interests you. It cannot help you directly with the course but it may help indirectly by developing your feel for the subject.

You don't need to make any detailed notes on this advance reference material unless you wish to, but a brief note of what it contains may help you later, and even save you searching through mountains of material to find something you require.

Recommended texts

Secondly, there are the **recommended texts** for a course. Several of these may be mentioned for your course, all containing information relevant to it. However, normally only one book will be used for most of the course, and this may be considered as the **core text**.

I would recommend you to **buy your own copy** if possible (unless provided for you). The rest can be referred to as necessary by borrowing from friends or studying them in libraries. These other texts may include useful material not contained for some reason in the core text, or have extra material, or approach it in a different way.

Of course, if money is no problem you may well wish to buy other texts, but this is normally unnecessary. If money is very tight you can usually get along quite well, even without buying the core text, particularly if you make a good set of class notes and get occasional access to the core texts when necessary.

Suggested extra reading
Thirdly, there is **suggested extra reading**. This is normally material not covered in the course, and not examined in the exam. Again, it is largely for the benefit of interested students who want a greater understanding of the subject, beyond the needs of the examination.

References may be made to various books or articles throughout the course. Always note these down in your class notes and deal with them as described elsewhere. Again, you won't normally have to buy any of this material.

"We'll swop you next year's grant for the whole place."

The process of getting extra tuition in a subject from someone other than your instructor outside class time is known as having **tutorials** (or, in Ireland, **grinds**).

Extra tuition has become a growing part of the education business. It is advertised in newspapers and on notice boards in schools, colleges, community centres and elsewhere. Quite a few students take extra tuition today, and many teachers earn a useful income from it.

Whether obtained free or at some cost it may be a useful part of one's study, or not, according to circumstances. Does such tuition reflect an inadequate education system, or does it fulfil a genuine need? These questions are outside the scope of this book — but the facility does exist, and you can use it.

Official tutorials

In colleges and universities official tutorial periods are often timetabled each week. A lecturer or postgraduate student may take a small number of students for more detailed discussion of lecture material. The student may find that he needs more individual tuition in some part of a topic. In this case the lecturer or instructor, whose lecture load is lighter than that of a school teacher, will usually be willing to spend some time with the student discussing his or her particular problem. Full use should be made of such help.

Private tuition

For students who are not in this lucky position, possibly in school where a teacher may not always have enough time, and who don't know anyone able to help them free of charge, then it may be possible to pay someone for extra tuition. The study problem may be solved in one or two hour-long sessions, but such a small problem could probably be dealt with by asking your instructor.

If several sessions are recommended or needed, then make sure you or your parents can afford the fee. It is no use booking six sessions, and only attending three because of lack of funds.

If you do proceed, find someone who is clearly **well qualified** to teach you what you want to know. If you are at school and preparing for school leaving exams, pick someone who has a **degree** in your subject, for example a degree in a science subject for a general science course, in chemistry for a chemistry course, or in history for a history course. For languages, such as French, a person without a degree but who can speak the language fluently could help you practise the language — which after all is the best way to learn a language.

If you are an undergraduate, then you need a postgraduate or someone with a higher degree in your own subject. Only they will have the real depth of understanding of the subject necessary.

Whoever you choose, they need to be convenient to you. It is no good if you have to spend an hour and a half travelling there and back for a one-hour session. They need to be able to be available as **frequently** as you need them, maybe two or three times a week, and at the **times** you need to fit in with your timetable. Tutors will often take several students in a small group to **share the cost**. This may not suit you, however, if you really want individual attention.

If you do go ahead, make sure you get what **you** need, and good value for your money. Extra tuition is not essential, and many students do perfectly well without it. But it does have its uses.

Do *You* Need Extra Tuition?

- ☐ Topics not taught in class?
- ☐ Missed lessons through illness or for other reasons?
- ☐ Lost important notes?
- ☐ Not sure of old notes?
- ☐ Trouble in understanding parts of the subject?
- ☐ An unsympathetic teacher, lecturer or college tutor?
- ☐ Need to talk through study problems?
- ☐ Difficulty in understanding technical English (overseas students)?
- ☐ Falling behind in studies?
- ☐ Need a different slant on the subject?
- ☐ Teachers/lecturers involved in industrial action?
- ☐ Can't master some of the basics?

You will have done a certain amount of studying on your subject throughout the course, but as the exams draw near and classes come to an end, now is the time for intensive revision.

The **time to start** this phase will depend on what level of exam you are studying for, the number of subjects you are taking, and the amount of material in each subject.

Intensive revision may be as little as a day or two for a single exam, to several weeks if several exams are to be taken together. As for myself, I allowed two weeks for GCE O-level, four weeks for GCE A-level, and six weeks for the University Final Degree Examination. You will have to decide **how much time** to allocate for yourself. Different students may need differing periods of time, the stronger student requiring less and the weaker student more. Make sure, however, that you leave enough time to cover all the material comfortably. Too much time is better than too little.

Planning a revision timetable

Write out a revision timetable for yourself (*see* example on the opposite page). Divide up the subjects about equally, according to the time available. You can adjust this somewhat if you feel the need to study a weaker subject more and a stronger one rather less. But don't neglect any subject too much. Make these decisions at the start — not later when precious time will have gone forever.

- For each subject divide up the whole subject matter into roughly equal sections, to equal the number of study periods you have allotted for the subject.
- Make a note on your timetable of the topics to be studied in each study period, to be sure of covering everything.

It is easy when dealing with numerous subjects and topics to overlook something. The timetable will now be the cornerstone of your revision plan. Keep it where you can quickly refer to it, and — most important of all — **stick to it!**

Rest days

When you are planning your timetable allow for a few rest days or half days in between. No-one can study effectively for days or weeks on end without a break. If necessary extend the whole programme a few days. Keep days off to a reasonable minimum but use them to full advantage, to relax, exercise, and give your brain a real rest from study.

	SUN	MON	TUES	WED	THUR	FRI	SAT	SUN
A M	PREPARATION ↑↓	CLASS	CLASS	CHEM. (org)	GEOG. (Amer)	CHEM. (Phys)	BIOL. (Bot)	DAY OFF
P M		CLASS	Geog. (Euro)	GEOG. (Euro)	MATHS. (Geom)	MATHS. (Alg)	ENG. LIT. (Poetry)	
E V E N		ENG. LIT. (play)	MATHS. (Geom)	BIOL. (Zool)	Night off	ENG. LIT. (Novel)	GEOG. (Aust)	

	MON	TUES	WED	THUR	FRI	SAT	SUN	MON
A M	CHEM. (Inorg)	ENG. LIT. (Novel)	CHEM. (Inorg)	GEOG. (Amer)	DAY OFF	Refresh Memory ↑↓		EXAMS START
P M	ENG. LIT. (Play)	CHEM. (org)	BIOL. (Ecol)	P.M. OFF	DAY OFF			
E V E N	BIOL (Bot)	night off	MATHS. (Arith)	BIOL. (Zool)				

Each subject – 5 sessions

MATHS	–Geometry 2	GEOGRAPHY	–Europe 2	ENG LIT	–Novel 2
	Algebra 2		America 2		Play 2
	Arithmetic 1		Australia 1		Poetry 1

CHEMISTRY	–Organic 2	BIOLOGY	–Botany 2
	Inorganic 2		Zoology 2
	Physical 1		Ecology 1

A specimen revision timetable

How Should I Study?

Everyone has a way of studying which suits them best, but a few words of advice may be helpful. Studying alone is usually best for intensive work, but in the early stages of revision, group study (officially or unofficially) may help you to compare viewpoints and thoroughly understand the material. For intensive study 100% concentration is vital.

Self-discipline

Discipline yourself to study for **set periods** (say three hours at a time), following your timetable strictly. Take short breaks in between. These will depend on what suits you best and your span of concentration. It might be a ten-minute coffee break in the middle, or five minutes at the end of each hour, or a couple of minutes at each half-hour.

Whatever you do, don't let the breaks get out of hand; keep them to a minimum. Take a longer break for lunch or your evening meal, for say an hour, and relax completely for this period before going back. Timetable these breaks. When you return for a new session, it can be helpful sometimes to change the subject and study something completely different.

A place to study

Have your own room, which must be quiet, away from the television, radio, traffic, or noise from younger children. If you cannot concentrate at home, try to arrange to study at a relative's or friend's home. Your school or college may have **study rooms** or **libraries** where you can study in peace, or you could use your local **public library**.

How to study

Do concentrate fully on your work. No matter how hard you may try, if the television or radio is on near you, or you are surrounded by chattering friends, the information your brain will be receiving will be a lethal mixture of study material and distractive junk. As a last resort, if you live in a flat near a railway station or over a disco, and have nowhere else to go, then consider **earplugs** (available from chemists) to cut out extraneous noise.

When you come to study, be well prepared and determined to do the job well. A half-hearted or reluctant approach will get you nowhere.

As you approach each subject

- check the syllabus to make sure you have covered (or will be covering) all it contains
- study the past papers for the last few years (*see* page 35) so that you know what to expect.

This may lead to some changes in your revision timetable, so deal with this as early as possible.

Tuning in

Having timetabled your work for a three-hour session, sit down and read through your study material — normally your class notes, but this may include a core text or other material. This allows your brain to tune into the subject and particular topic . Human beings seem to have different ways of thinking about different subjects, for example maths or history, and you need to get on the right wavelength for the particular subject. Try to make sure you really understand what you are reading and *think* about it where necessary. Reading it aloud can be surprisingly helpful.

Writing out the key points

The second, more important and longer part of the process, is to **write out** the material in the form of **revision notes**. These are not the same as your more detailed course notes, but rather brief notes of the key points. These key points will be invaluable later, as we shall see.

Most topics can be simply reduced to a few pages of revision notes, and this should be your aim. Write down the major points as you work through the topic using

- abbreviations
- your own shorthand methods (*see* page 18)
- phrases and keywords

to help you recall later what you have been studying. This physical writing-down process seems to imprint knowledge on the brain much more firmly than simply reading; you will also have two independent inputs of the same material. You will find in the examination room, too, that having recently written out the material in brief note form it is easier to recall and write out again more fully. If **maps or diagrams** are involved, sketch them out briefly for practice. If **calculations** are involved do several **examples** to get the feel of them and make sure you really can do them.

Read through

Finally, to finish and lock the material in your mind, read through the revision notes you have just made. Make sure that

- you can read and make sense of them — you will need to later
- they are a reasonable summary of the material you have just studied. This gives you a *third* chance of going over the material.

Now take a break.

Follow this routine for all sections of your subjects as far as you can. Then, at the end of your revision period, you will have a *full* set of revision notes for *all* your subjects.

Finally, timetable your revision to finish two or three days before the first examination, and take a full day off before starting the final lap.

Am I Taking Too Many Subjects?

Consider your aims

For students taking only one or two subjects, it is usually necessary for them to pass each and every exam paper. The same can be true, of course, for those studying several at once. But in some cases students may find themselves studying a subject towards an examination which they do not absolutely need to pass, and which is a subject they find great difficulty with or have no interest in.

This particularly applies to students still at school, taking certain subjects in which they had no choice. A student may be studying eight subjects when he/she only has to pass in five to pass the examination overall.

In Ireland, for example, this is the case where a pass in five subjects is needed to gain the Leaving Certificate; better grades or results may be obtained by passing more of the subjects studied, but it is not *absolutely* necessary to pass more than five actually to gain the Certificate.

Admittedly whilst it is better to pass as many examinations as possible and to get better grades in as many subjects as possible, it can happen that a student is faced with a subject he cannot get to grips with, has no interest in and no use for, has no hope of passing and does not really *need* to pass anyway no matter how hard he tries. In this case there is no point in wasting any time on that subject. *Time* is the student's most precious commodity in the examination season; to waste it on such a 'lost cause' when it could be better spent on other subjects is pointless. It would have been better to drop that subject, perhaps in favour of studying something more useful, but this is not always possible.

The 'lost cause'

I illustrate the point with my own experience at the age of 15 facing GCE O-level exams. I was studying eight subjects, some by choice and others not. With a heavy revision workload I came to English Literature — not one of my favourite subjects, to say the least. I was heading for a science career. As well as several science subjects I was studying Maths and English Language (vital for progress in any sphere), plus Geography (in which I was interested), and French (which I thought would be useful). English Literature, however, held nothing for me at all. Some people enjoy and do well in English Literature — each to his own — but poetry left me cold, the play we studied was Shakespeare's *Macbeth*, whose intricacies I could never fathom, and Dickens' *David Copperfield*, a massive work; whilst it had been interesting to read during the course, the prospect of revising this was daunting in the extreme.

I decided that English Literature was for me a write-off. It would have taken more than my whole revision period to sort this subject out, and I would probably still have failed. Instead, I did not spend any revision time at all on English Literature. I went into the exam room, filled in my name, handed in a blank paper, and left. I *used the time* on my other seven subjects and did well in them. I even passed French, about which I was doubtful, probably thanks to the extra time available. This calculated failure has had no adverse effect on my subsequent career.

"I think I'll have to give A-Level Chinese a miss."

Caution

There is a note of caution, however. This should not be treated as an *excuse* simply to forget about one or more subjects, but is a highly calculated, reasoned evaluation of the position, designed to *maximise* results, and only applies in certain special cases.

Under the rules and regulations of your examination, you *may* have to go along to the exam (in which you have no interest), just to be ticked off as present, or to hand in a blank paper with your name on it, or to be present for the first half-hour before leaving. These rules are for administrative reasons, and if you do not comply penalties may result.

Don't just fail to turn up for the exam: find out beforehand exactly what the rules and procedures are and abide by them. After leaving the exam room, use the rest of the morning or afternoon constructively to revise for your next paper.

Try not to enter more examinations than you can properly revise for. If this does happen, do not sacrifice good subjects for bad (*see* previous section). A variation of the 'lost cause' however may be possible for certain students. There may be students who feel that they have too much on their plate to sit all their subjects at one go, but would still like to pass *all* their subjects, and not drop one (or more) as a lost cause.

Re-sits

Examination re-sits are sometimes available (normally in the autumn for summer exams, and so on). In any case the exams will be held again the following year. It may well pay a student studying say eight subjects to sit only six of these at the first attempt, and take the other two (along with any re-sits) later in the year or next year.

It may be possible to do this officially by only registering for say six exams. If this is not possible, you may be able to do it unofficially by entering for eight, but only seriously trying for six and not wasting any time on the other two. After further work and study on those two subjects, without the pressure of the other six as well, they can be re-sat and (hopefully) passed in the re-sits or the following year.

With some subjects studied later in life, at home or college, an examination can often be taken in **stages** as study progresses. Accountancy examinations, for example, may be taken in several parts or stages over a period of years if necessary, not all in one go. Some students may prefer this option, if available.

"Actually it's my eighth re-sit!"

Getting hold of past papers

Well before the examination, get hold of the past papers for the previous five years (if you can) for each subject you intend to take. These are normally available from the Examination Board, or from your school or college. In cases of difficulty your instructor should be able to tell you where to get them.

Anticipation

A study of past papers will be very useful to you in taking your exam. It will make you more aware of what to expect, and help you to do certain preparations beforehand, such as **working out timing and marks**. It is much easier to tackle an exam when you know in advance what time and marks will be allowed, than if you have no idea what to expect.

Analysis

Carry out a really thorough analysis of each set of past papers. The time to do this is just before you begin serious revision for that subject; it will then be fresh in your mind as you study.

If the **format** of the papers has been the same (over the last five years), the chances are that it will be the same again, and you can plan on that basis. Make a mental note of

- the number of questions you will have to answer,
- the total time period allowed for the exam, and
- the total number of questions on the paper.

Note any particular instructions.

- How many **sections** are involved (if more than one)?
- How many questions are in each section, and how many questions will you have to answer from each section?
- Are there any special instructions to be followed, or special questions, e.g. a compulsory question or a multiple choice question?

Write this down in note form on a sheet of paper as a *Past Paper Analysis* and pin it up next to your timetable for easy reference later (*see* the example on the next page).

Knowing **how many** questions must be answered lets you plan the timing for each question *beforehand*. This will save you valuable time in the exam. It also gives you an idea of **how long** your answers should be. For example, three questions in three hours (one hour each) will mean lengthy detailed answers, whereas nine questions in 2½ hours (15 minutes each with 15 minutes to spare) will mean only fairly brief answers are required.

SUBJECT	NUMBER OF QUESTIONS TO BE ANSWERED	TOTAL NUMBER OF QUESTIONS ON PAPER	TIME (hours)	TIME ALLOWED FOR READING PAPER (mins)	TIME PER QUESTION (mins)	SPARE TIME AT END (mins)	SPECIAL INSTRUCTIONS / COMMENTS
GENERAL SCIENCE	6	12	3	—	30	—	3 sections (phys, chem, biol) 4 questions in each section, answer 2 from each (i.e.) 2/4 , 2/4 , 2/4
FRENCH	5	7	3	(5)	35	—	—
MATHS	1 + 4	6	3	—	60/30	—	Multiple choice has 1/3 time, 1/3 marks
HISTORY	5	7	3	(5)	35	—	Q.1. Compulsory
GEOGRAPHY	5	8	3	(5)	35	—	2 sections, answer 2 from each + 1 other from either section, (i.e.) A 2/4 , B 2/4 + 1
ART	4	6	2½	(5)	35	(5)	Answer 2 from section A – 2/3, Answer 2 from section B – 2/3, Section C not applicable
ENGLISH	5	5	2¼	(5)	25	(5)	Answer all questions.

An example of past paper analysis

A choice of questions

Knowing how many questions there will be, and what choice you will have (for example, six questions from eight, or five questions from nine) may influence your study or revision. For example, if a large choice is offered it may be that you need not to have studied all the syllabus for some reason and there will be questions on the paper that you will not be able to, or even should not, attempt to do. Sometimes this will apply to whole sections. Don't let this put you off. The questions or sections are put there for other students who have covered different areas or topics. Your instructor will guide you on this if necessary.

In a university maths examination, for example, questions may be set for those students studying maths to **Honours** degree level, and for **Pass** degrees, and as a subsidiary subject — all on the same paper. You are only expected to answer, and should only attempt, those questions for your particular level. If you are not clear in the examination which questions you are supposed to do, then *ask*! Make a mental note of any such variations you are likely to meet; jot them down on your analysis sheet.

Looking at past questions

Having sorted out the format, take a closer look at the questions themselves. You could

- make a separate analysis sheet for each subject or
- write notes on your general analysis sheet if it is not too complicated.

(The former system is usually best; the general analysis sheet is for instant reference, and shouldn't need detailed study to see what information you want from it.)

In the study of questions, work out **how many** questions there are per topic (or per instructor). Notice how the **choice** falls over these; if you have one very bad topic can you avoid it totally if necessary? Notice the **style** of each question on each topic. When the same person sets questions over a number of years, you may be able to detect similarities in the questions from year to year, and discover favourite areas or topics examined and questions asked in particular ways. Concentrate on these areas in your study; make sure you know them well — but not at the expense of the rest of your course naturally. After all, this year may be the year of change. Different instructors (on different topics) set questions in different ways and with different emphasis. Knowing the style of a particular question will help you to answer it better.

Frequency of certain topics

Notice how *often* topics come up from year to year. If a topic (or part of a topic) has come up every year it could well come up again. If a topic has only ever appeared once in five years it is unlikely to come up (but this may be the year it reappears).

Look out, in the case of particular topics, for the favourite ways in which they are asked. What specific areas *within* that topic are most often asked? Is the topic examined through

- diagrams to be drawn, or provided to be labelled
- or by calculation
- or some other method?
- Are most (or all) questions the single essay type, or are they mainly intermediate types (*see* page 42)?
- Do multiple-part questions cover the whole subject, or just one topic?

"There's nothing in here about the first law of thermodynamics."

Sometimes the whole subject is examined in brief by a compulsory multiple-part question, or an examiner may set a multiple-part question on his own topic. Is there any further choice within the question, and is this *always* the case, or only *sometimes*?

Work out the **number of marks** per question and per part question if the papers follow a uniform pattern. This again will save you time in the exam room, and is good practice anyway. Be particularly aware of any special marking schemes (e.g. 1 question worth 40% and 6 questions worth 10% each). Try to get the 'flavour' of the questions.

Changes in examination format

If changes have been made on the papers over the past five years then paper analysis becomes less reliable, but it is still valuable. If there have been only minor changes in format, then this does not make much difference. If major changes have taken place regularly (which is rare), the exercise is of little value as to format, but still worth doing to get the flavour of the questions.

Sometimes one can detect a change in style of question, possibly as a result of a different person setting the questions. If changes have taken place, remember that the most recent papers are the most reliable, the older ones less so. (If a major change occurred three years ago, but none since then, use only the last three years' past papers; ignore the older ones.)

If a change in format happened the previous year then use last year's paper as a guide to format; it is unlikely to change again, and use *all* the papers for a guide to the flavour of the questions. A certain amount of common sense needs to be applied to this process.

Warning

Although past paper analysis is certainly valuable, to suggest what will be coming in the way of format and style and choice of question, DO NOT TAKE THESE FOR GRANTED. Always be prepared for a change in any of these factors. They do change from time to time; even if they have never changed before. *This may be the year of change.* Be mentally prepared, and don't go into the exam room rigidly expecting something only to be totally thrown off balance by change.

If change does occur don't worry too much. You will still be able to do the exam. See *what* has changed; work out new timing and marks as quickly as you can. Read and comply with any different instructions, then carry on and deal with the questions as your normally would.

Preparing for different types of question

In an examination, marks may be won or lost depending on the **type** of question answered, quite apart from the **knowledge** a student may or may not have. Where a **choice** of question is given, and the student has sufficient knowledge to take full advantage of that choice, it becomes very important to make full use of that choice. In other words, choose the questions where you can win the most **marks** — (this may not be the same as those questions you *know* most about).

Usually the best question to answer is the one you feel very knowledgeable and confident about. Make this your first question to tackle and the next most knowledgeable your second, and so on. But be aware of the problems and advantages of the various *types* of questions and work this to your own advantage.

Broadly questions fall into three main types, with variations in each category. The main types are:

- ● Multiple-part questions
- ● Segmented (intermediate type) questions
- ● Essay (single-answer type) questions

A number of examples will illustrate the various types.

Multiple-part questions are of two main kinds — those offering the candidate an internal choice within the question, and those which offer no choice.

Questions with an internal choice

For example, *Answer 8 of the following:* (with a list of 12 short questions). This is probably the easiest of all questions to answer. Each part will gain a small point. It needs only one (or very few) words to answer each part. These questions are usually drawn from a wide range of the subject giving everyone a good chance of finding 8 bits to answer. Full marks will be given for a correct answer, or none if wrong (e.g. 2½ marks each, out of 20). Half marks may be given if half right. It is easy to pick up plenty of marks quickly with this type of question.

This type of question is also well worth answering as maybe a third, fourth or fifth question, even if you can only answer say 6 out of 12. It is still possible to get 15 marks — a very good mark for any one complete question. It is also a good last question if none other is available to you, even if you know very little. Even 1/12 will guarantee you 2½ marks, and 2/12 will give you 5 very valuable marks.

Questions without an internal choice

For example, *Answer all the following:* (list of 8 short questions). You are required to attempt *all* the questions. This can still be an excellent question if you know quite a few answers, since they are *quick* to do and *easy* to pick up marks on. As with the previous example this is a useful third, fourth or fifth question when you know 5 or 6 points definitely, or as a last resort knowing only one or two points.

As for the last example and all other examples, *time* the question carefully (*see* page 52). For a 30-minute question of eight parts, each part will be four minutes maximum (32 minutes maximum overall) and for a 20-minute question 2½ minutes maximum. You should get most of your answers down much faster than this, and so gain valuable time (which is another important feature of this type of question) to spend on other questions.

Questions not initially apparent as multiple-part questions

Another example would at first seem to belong in the second category of segmented questions. But closer examination of the question shows multiple answers in most segments, and so we can look on it as a multiple-part (with or without internal choice) question.

We'll look at an example on the next page.

Answer 4 of the following:

	Marks	*(e.g. $4 \times 6 = 24 + 1 = 25$)*
(a) (i) to (vi)	6 x 1	(total 6)
(b) (i) to (iv)	4 x 1½	(total 6)
(c) Illustrate the truth and limitations		
of . . .	2 x 3	(total 6)
(d) Write notes on . . .	6	(total 6)
(e) Write notes on . . .	6	(total 6)
(f) Write down . . .		
Discuss changes if . . .	2 x 3	(total 6)

This question has 16 separate points or questions. It offers plenty of choice, allowing odd marks to be picked up here and there even if your knowledge is sketchy. If you can *write notes on* . . . one of the topics (requiring 20 minutes divided by 4 = 5 minutes, or 25 minutes divided by 4 = 6 minutes, and so on) of about a paragraph or a third to half a page, then 4 to 6 valuable marks can be won. But if not, you could avoid (d) and (e) completely. Don't forget, 'notes' are just that — a long essay is *not* asked for. If time is short a series of phrases will usually do.

Note

Part (c) asks for *'truths and limitations'*. Make sure you give *both* sides. If only the limitations are discussed then only half marks are possible.

In Part (f) half the marks will be for putting down the initial situation and the other half will be for the situation after change. Make sure you consider and answer *both* parts. The marks may be split 4 + 2 if the former is more important than the latter, or even 5 + 1 if the change is a minor one. In the last case however 5 marks are well worth having; the one lost won't make much difference if you don't know what happens after whatever changes are made.

Segmented Questions

Segmented questions are normally good ones to answer. Marks can be gained quickly by answering the various parts of the question. Answers are *not* called for in the same depth as for essay questions. Each part of the answer will normally take half a page to a page at the most.

Timing is critical with the segmented question. Marks may be allocated unevenly, and you need to avoid wasting a lot of time on the smaller sections at the expense of the bigger ones where most of the marks are. Let's look at some examples.

Questions with internal choice
'Answer 3 of the following' or *'4 of the following 6.'*

Questions with no internal choice
'Answer all the following.' [with a list of 3, 4 or 5 pieces]:

Similar comments apply as for multiple-part questions, but this type can be harder to answer, needing one or more paragraphs for each part. It is not as easy to pick up loose marks with these questions, and they take longer to answer. If no internal choice is available the question becomes rather more difficult again (unless of course you know all the answers!). If most of the sections are further subdivided it should be considered as a multiple-part question.

Another question with no internal choice

Question 8.
Describe how . . . and explain what happens when . . . Give one example of . . . and one of . . .   Starting from . . . how would you (a) . . . (b) . . .

Although it does not say so, this question is really:

1. (i) & (ii)
2. (i) & (ii)
3. (i) & (ii)

It would probably be marked as 6 x 3 = 18, plus 2 at the discretion of the marker (total 20 marks). In these examples the marks are evenly spread, and so you should spend equal time on each section. But marks are *not* always evenly spread. For example, suppose you had allowed yourself twenty minutes to answer this question:

Question 9.
Define . . .   (2 marks)
Outline methods for . . .   (10 marks)
Calculate . . .   (4 marks)
What are . . .   (4 marks)

The bulk of the marks (half the total) are for the second section, to which you should therefore allot half your time (10 minutes). Only a couple of minutes should be given to writing out the definition. If you simply can't remember it after two minutes, leave it out and move on to the next section. Each part of the question is independent, although the whole question relates to the same topic. Even if the whole question cannot be answered, you can still gain valuable marks by doing parts of this question as a last resort towards the end of the exam.

Questions with interdependent answers

Another kind of segmented question involves dependency. For example:

Question 10.
Define . . . and . . .
By means of sketch graphs [not on graph paper]
show qualitatively . . . and then for (a) . . . and (b) . . .
Using the graphs deduce (1) . . . (2) . . .
Calculate . . .

This asks you to show something for a main case, and two special cases. For each case you will need to use what you have done to derive two pieces of information. Finally you need to calculate something based on what you have deduced.

Do not choose this question unless you are confident about the *whole* question. Although it looks like many parts, and marks are to be had for each one, answers for each bit will depend on your previous answers, and will be needed for subsequent parts. If you cannot answer the first part then you will soon run into trouble with the whole thing, and waste precious time. The only loose marks here are for the definition which is hardly worth bothering about if you can't manage the rest.

This type of question crops up very often in Maths and similar subjects, where you have to calculate or prove something in order to calculate or prove something else. Be *wary* of these questions, and be sure of getting the first part right or the whole question is lost.

Notice the question in the example says 'by *sketch* graphs' and '*qualitatively*', in other words in a descriptive manner. You are not asked (in this case) to draw accurate graphs on graph paper in a *quantitative* manner. You will only waste your own time doing this.

This third category is probably the hardest of all for most students to answer. As you are only writing about one topic for the whole of your answer, it can be hard to decide what to put in or leave out, or how much to write. Basically, **time the question**. Write as much as you can in the time you have allotted yourself. Stick to the **main points first**, getting across your main arguments, backed up with **examples**, and then go on to discuss the minor ones. Make notes in the margin if you feel it will be helpful (cross them out afterwards).

Don't waffle on aimlessly — it simply won't get you any marks. Stick to the question actually asked, and write only on what is asked for. This last point is sometimes difficult as little guidance may be given in the question itself.

A choice

You may be asked, for example, to *'Discuss (a) or (b)'*. This is a *single* essay. Do not answer (a) AND (b). If you do both and spend half the time on each you may only get half marks maximum for say (a), and (b) will not be marked *at all* no matter how well or badly you have done in (a).

The various types in this category are:

Question 1.
[A long section of data or information]. *Discuss.*

This is probably the easiest type in this section; you have been given plenty to go on in the question, and can see what is wanted.

Question 2.
Compare and contrast . . . or
Show differences and similarities of . . .

Again, this is one of the easier types of essay question. You know exactly what is being asked for. You might be able to use a **tabular** form of answer, especially if time is short. Your list or table can be expanded by several paragraphs of **text** dealing with each point in turn.

The short question

For example:

What if . . . or *Describe how . . .* [only a couple of sentences with little information are given].

These types are more difficult. Only a little information is given as to what is sought. Again, cover the main points you can think of first, and develop them in more detail as time permits.

The 'general' essay question

Examples:

> *Discuss the meaning of innocence.*
> *Write an essay on fair play.*

No information is given in the question. These types of question are best avoided if possible. They are probably the hardest to answer well, and the most difficult to produce marks unless you really **know your subject**, and can **organise your ideas** properly. If you do, then by all means go ahead, but if you are unsure — beware! Let's take some further examples:

> Question 12. *'History repeats itself.' Discuss.*
> Question 13. *Write an essay on the value of art.*

The range of such topics can be very broad indeed. You could spend days or even weeks writing on the last two questions and still not 'answer' the question being asked. These are extreme examples, and questions are seldom this broad. But it illustrates the point. If you have some **inside information** (such as which instructor set the question, or which part of the syllabus the question refers to), this could help you narrow down the question and make it easier to answer.

Tips on writing good essays
● **Think** before you start writing.
● Jot down a few **ideas** or **arguments** you would like to get across.
● Don't just give one point of view — discuss **more than one**.
● Remember sometimes that the examiner may not be interested in the actual conclusions, but in the **way you express ideas**.
● When you have thought what ideas and arguments to express, **then** back them up with facts.
● Make a simple **essay plan**, with each paragraph establishing a new point. You can plan each paragraph as: (a) an opening statement, idea or argument (b) a development of various pros and cons (c) a factual back-up to points previously made (d) a conclusion.
● Ensure your essay has a definite **structure** i.e. a beginning, middle and an end.

Multiple Choice Questions should not be confused with multiple *part* questions. Increasingly, examinations have developed the MCQ format as part of, or even the whole of, an examination. It consists of a series of short questions, each with a number of alternative printed answers (usually 3 to 5), one of which the student has to tick off as the correct one. For example:

What is the average walking pace of a human adult?

1 mph	
4 mph	
14 mph	
40 mph	

What is the general speed limit for cars in towns?

10 mph	
20 mph	
30 mph	
40 mph	

These types of questions or exams should be fairly easy to deal with. After all, **the answer is there** in front of you somewhere; it is just a question of finding it. Sometimes **penalties** are given (minus marks) for incorrect answers, to stop guesswork. If this is the case, and you don't know the answer, it is better to leave the space blank (getting zero) rather than guess incorrectly (getting minus 1).

Sometimes the instructions tell you to **underline** the correct answer or to **cross out** what is incorrect. Be very careful indeed to follow these instructions; confusion may arise when marking if you do not. For example:

Underline the correct answer: 5, ~~10~~, 15, 20.

Here the candidate has crossed out what he thinks is the correct answer, but he has underlined nothing. Or again:

5, <u>10</u>, <u>15</u>, 20.

Here the candidate has underlined *two* answers, as he/she is not sure which of these is right, but knows one of them is.

Some Multiple Choice Questions

Notes

1. Cross out the incorrect answers:
   Cross out 3 leaving
   (a) Paris is the capital of Germany.
   the correct one
   (b) France is the capital of Italy.
   (c) Moscow is the capital of Russia.
   (d) New York is the capital of America.

2. Underline the correct answer:
   The Russian Revolution happened in: Underline only
   (a) 1717   one statement.
   (b) 1817
   (c) 1917
   (d) 1945

3. Tick which statement is *incorrect*:
   (a) red and yellow mixed give orange   Tick wrong
   (b) red and yellow mixed give blue   statement.
   (c) blue and yellow mixed give green
   (d) black and white mixed give grey

4. Tick which statement is correct:
   A Multiple Choice Question means you can: Tick right
   (a) answer any question   statement.
   (b) give more than one answer
   (c) give only one answer

5. Underline the correct answer: Underline only
   Michael Faraday was a   one statement.
   (a) Novelist
   (b) Explorer
   (c) Scientist
   (d) Cross-Channel swimmer
   (e) Aviator

6. Tick the word which is mis-spelled: Tick wrong
   (a) Dissipate   statement.
   (b) Definite
   (c) Derivative
   (d) Derisory
   (e) Dirigable

There are a number of special types of examination question which should be considered. These include:

Further choice questions
For example:

> **Question 4.** *Answer (A) or (B):*
> $$(A) \ldots$$
> $$(B) \ldots$$

This type of question has been touched on earlier, under essay questions, but it can occur in any category. It is really two questions in one. It is good for the candidate, since it increases the overall **choice** on the paper (say giving 6 questions out of 9 instead of only 6 out of 8). It happens when an examiner, who may only have one question to set, wants to broaden the scope of his question, and so splits it into two separate ones dealing with different areas of his course. This should be considered as a bonus — but remember, you cannot do *both* parts.

Mixed questions
For example:

> **Question 2.**
> *Give an account of* . . .   (10 marks)
> *How would you* . . . *3 of the following* [from 5].   (3 x 5 marks)

This is a mixture of an essay and a segmented question (with internal choice) with an even spread of marks. It should be timed and dealt with accordingly. To take another example:

> **Question 7.**
> *Discuss in a comparative way* . . .   (20 marks)
> *Comment briefly on*
>   *(a) structure of P_4O_{10} molecules in the gas phase*   (2 marks)
>   *(b) surface structure of BeO crystals*   (2 marks)
>   *(c)* . . .   (2 marks)
>   *(d)* . . .   (2 marks)
>   *(e)* . . .   (2 marks)

This one is a mixture of an essay question and a multiple part (*without* internal choice). As most of the marks (two-thirds) are going on the essay part it is best treated as an essay-type question when you are choosing question type. In this case two-thirds of the time available should be given to the essay and a third to the rest (with a fifth of a third of the total time to each small part). As a last resort 10 marks could be obtained from the second part of the question, even if little attempt is made at the essay.

Note

You may know plenty about the structure of P_4O_{10} molecules as a liquid or solid, but this in itself will get you *no* marks, since the important word is 'gas'. Also, you may know a lot about BeO crystals in general, or about their internal structure — again *no* marks. The marks are only for what you know about the structure 'on the surface'. Once again, read the question very carefully and answer only what is asked for. Anything else will be a waste of your time.

Short essay questions

For example:

Question 1.
Write short accounts of both (a) . . . and (b) . . .

Note: (a) *and* (b), not (a) *or* (b).

This question is really two shorter essays, whether on related or different topics. Treat each one separately. Allow half the total time for each half. As a last resort, if you know nothing about one half, remember that half a question is better than none, provided you can do one half well (or reasonably well). It can still help you towards that vital pass mark. Again:

Question 2.
How might the facts be accounted for:
(a) . . .
(b) . . .
Suggest further methods for . . .

This, too, is really a two-essay question, and not a multi-part question. First, account for the facts in (a), and suggest further methods for (a) as one half of the question (i.e. one short essay). Then do the same for (b) as the other short essay.

The vague question

An example from a physical chemistry paper of some years ago will illustrate the problems of this type of question:

Question 3. *Answer 4 of the following 8 parts:*
(a)   *Outline in about half a page any recent developments in physical chemistry which you regard as of special significance or importance at the present time.*
(b)   *. . . , etc to (h).*

This is a very vague part-question. It would be best to avoid it, treating the whole question as having only seven parts and answering four from the more factual parts (b) to (h).

Other Types of Question

The vague question (continued)

This vague type of question sometimes forms the whole of a question, and is again better avoided. They are really essay-type questions, with no information for you to build on. Other examples would be:

What do you think about . . . or
Develop your own ideas on . . .

Such questions are fine in relaxed class discussions for broadening the mind and getting a wider perspective of the subject. But for a student trying to pass an exam they are very risky indeed. You have no idea of what is really being asked for, and you are often asked to give your own theory which may or may not be acceptable from the examiner's point of view. All three viewpoints (yours, the examiner's and the marker's) may be different and equally possible or correct, but you are at the whim of others for your marks. This type of question tends to occur a great deal in arts subjects. Students taking subjects known for this type of question (literature, art appreciation, philosophy etc.) should seek specialist advice from their instructors or tutors.

Alternative formats

Sometimes papers will fall outside the normal run of formats.

Example 1 — Paper in Physics

Instructions

Answer as many questions as possible.
Start answers to each question on a separate paper. Questions do not all carry equal marks. Answers should be short (no more than a few lines).
Questions:

(1) a, b, c	*(4) a & b*	*(7) a & b*
(2) a & b	*(5) a, b, c, d, e*	*(8) a & b*
(3) a, b, c	*(6) a, b, c, d, e*	*(9) a, b, c*
(27 sections)		

You are expected (it can be assumed) to answer all nine questions for full marks. But how do you *time* your answers? You could assume that each of the nine questions carries equal marks and allot equal time for each one. Or you could assume that each *part* question carries equal marks (i.e. 100 divided by 27) and so divide the total time by 27 for each part.

You can only judge this by looking at the various parts and considering whether they are all about equal. Do they all seem to require about the same amount of answer, or would some sections need longer answers than others? It is probable here as the questions don't carry equal marks that the individual sections or parts *do*. I would consider the instructions and information for this exam to be inadequate, but you may have to live with that.

Example 2 — Paper in Biology

Write about at least three and not more than five of the following topics. The number of topics attempted will not affect the total possible mark. (8 topics given).

Again you are in a quandary! What to do for the best? Answer three questions extensively and hopefully well — or answer five less extensively and hope to get an overall good mark? You may think this hard to answer, but it is even harder to mark. How can one balance out various students who may have done three, four or five questions, and give each one a mark out of 100 so as to reflect their ability, having regard to other candidates?

I don't see the sense in this format, except that it allows students who have studied a narrower range in greater depth, or a broader range in lesser depth, to have the same chance. In the former case you would presumably answer three and in the latter five questions. However, this is rarely the case where all students are studying the same course.

Otherwise your choice would depend on the type and area of each question and how you can relate to each one. It really is a question of 'see how you go'. Answer three questions first, anyway, on separate papers. See how the time is going. Timing is not too important since the number of questions you answer will not affect your final mark. Having finished go back over the three questions and improve them as far as you can. Time permitting, go on and do a fourth as well as you possibly can, checking it over carefully when finished. Then, and only then, tackle a fifth if there is still time.

But don't worry if you don't get the fourth or fifth done. The most important thing (after making sure you do three) is the *quality* of what you have done, not the *quantity*. Half questions or parts of questions are no good here, either. The mark will be given overall on what you have completed and the breadth and depth of your knowledge.

In general

In general, the longer the question the more useful information it gives you. So never be afraid of long questions. They are usually easier to tackle. Read the question *carefully*, and comply with *all* instructions both at the beginning and throughout the paper.

You should know beforehand the total time allowed for your exam. You also obviously know that the whole exam carries 100% marks — though not necessarily 100 marks as such — the paper may be marked out of more or less than 100 marks for convenience and all marks later converted to a percentage.

Going for the marks
Be prepared as far as possible before the exam, and during the exam, to **ration your time** to maximise your marks. You will probably know how many questions you will have to answer on the paper, either from looking at past papers (*see* page 35), or from the *Rules and Regulations*, or you may be told by your instructor. This will let you plan beforehand exactly how much time to spend on each question. Stick to this as far as possible. Allow five minutes at the start of the exam, if you can, to **read through the whole paper**.

● Set yourself different times for different questions where they carry different amounts of marks.

When working out the time per question, convert the total time to minutes and divide by the number of questions you will answer. Reduce this time if necessary to the nearest five minutes. This will give you a reasonable time per question. Multiply this by the number of questions again, and subtract from the total time to give the amount of *spare* time. A few examples will make this clearer:

Example 1
Five questions in 3 hours: (180 minutes ÷ 5 = 36 minutes per question).

Reduce this to 35 minutes per question. It is easier and quicker in the exam to calculate and operate time to the nearest five minutes — the odd minute is not critical. So:

35 minutes x 5 = 175; 180 minus 175 = 5 minutes to read the paper before you start. Make a note on your Past Paper Analysis Sheet: *5 minutes to start, plus 5 x 35 minutes (or (5), 5 x 35.)*

Sometimes the time per question is an exact division of the total time for the number of questions. This can be dealt with in two ways (Examples 2 and 3):

Example 2

Six questions in 3 hours: (180 ÷ 6 = 30 minutes per question).

No allowance is made for the first five minutes, but you should take this time anyway in the exam. Remember then you have to make up five minutes somewhere. Normally this is best done on the later questions. You may find you spend 30 minutes on the first three questions, and that the remaining three are two of 28 minutes and one of 27 minutes (173 minutes total time taken). With the initial five minutes used at the start this gives 178 minutes, leaving you two minutes to check the paper at the end.

Example 3

Five questions in 2½ hours: (150 ÷ 5 = 30 minutes per question).

Again the situation arises where the time/question is an exact division of the total time allowed. Allowing five minutes initially means reducing the remaining time (145 ÷ 5 = 29 minutes) to the nearest five minutes (25 minutes) leaves a lot of spare time at the end (20 minutes) *i.e. 5, 5 x 25, 20*. You can work on 25 minutes per question, and use the extra time available during the exam at your discretion, for the more difficult or lengthy questions. Either of the last two examples are quite acceptable. Another example would be:

Example 4

Nine questions in 2½ hours: (150 ÷ 9 = 16.67 minutes per question).

Allow 15 minutes per question: 15 x 9 = 135 minutes; 135 + 5 minutes initially = 140 minutes; 150 - 140 = 10 minutes to spare at the end, *i.e. (5), 9 x 15, (10)*.

Don't worry about an odd minute, but try to stick to the overall scheme and you will not run out of time. Keep an eye on your scheme as you go along. If you finish one question early you will have more time for the others, and be able to modify the scheme as you proceed. An extra minute or two will appear here and there, particularly towards the end of the paper. So, even if you haven't allowed for it in your calculation, you will often have a few minutes at the end to finish off questions or check through your answers.

These examples all assume that questions will carry equal marks, and so deserve equal amounts of time; but this is not always the case. Where questions are given different amounts of marks, time should be allotted **in proportion to the marks available**.

A question may be compulsory or carry more marks than the rest. If so, more time should be allowed.

Example 5

Answer Question 1 and any 3 others (Question 1 carries 40% of the marks).

In other words, one of 40% and three of 20% each. *Time 2½ hours.* Time this as:

Q. 1 — 1 hour and 3 questions of half an hour each.

Take the five minutes initially and make allowance for this somewhere (for example allowing 55 minutes to Question 1 and coming back to it later if necessary).

You can further divide your time *within* the various questions, in proportion to the marks available. In some cases the number of marks per question or part thereof is shown, but even if it is not, it is not hard to work it out roughly. Practise doing this exercise before the exam on past papers.

Example 6

Question: Answer 8 of the following:

		Answers
(a)	*What is a substance made only of one type of atom called?*	Element
(b)	*What is the smallest charged particle called?*	Electron
(c)	*How does a plant take in water?*	Through its roots
(d)	*What gas do plants absorb in photosynthesis?*	Carbon dioxide (CO_2)
(e)	*How does light and sound travel?*	In waves
(f)	*What is the chemical formula for water?*	H_2O
(g)	*What is the normal body temperature?*	98.4°F
(h)	...	
(i)	...	
etc.		

This is typical of the multiple-part question. It will probably be marked out of 20, i.e. 8 x 2½ marks; (or out of 25, 8 x 3 = 24, with students getting 24 being given 25). Each answer will get 2½ marks if correct. Notice that only one or two words are needed for each answer to get full marks. No more marks are available, *no matter how much more you write!*

Example 7

'Discuss the life and work of . . .' or
'Write an essay on . . .'

In essay-type questions the whole 20 (or whatever) marks are given on the whole question. The marker is usually looking for **specific points** which must be included to win the marks. Typically there will be 20 points worth 1 each, or perhaps 8 points worth 2 marks each with 4 for showing an understanding of the topic. In some subjects, however, the marker may simply give an **impression mark** out of 20 (say) as to what he feels is the overall value of the essay. You are at the mercy of the marker in this case, which is why this type of question is best avoided if possible.

When estimating the number of marks per question, or part question, it does not matter *how many* marks you use as a base to work from. What matters is the *proportions*. Examiners normally provide marking schemes which are so divided that the papers are quick and easy to mark, even if the totals do not add up to 100. For example, 4 parts of 5 marks each gives 20 marks per question, and six questions gives a total of 120.

Follow the instructions

Part or all of a question may require you to make a diagram or drawing. Always read and follow the instructions carefully. **Give what is asked for**, and don't waste precious time doing what is *not* asked for.

For example, you may be given a full page blank map in a geography exam. You may be asked to fill in the features such as mountain ranges and rivers, and name cities and countries. Give only what is *directly* asked for. Don't try to fill in the name of every town, for instance.

Colouring

Coloured pencils may help you show different features, but remember to draw a **colour code** in the margin or in a blank space to explain your use of colour, e.g. black for mountains, blue for rivers, red dots for cities. Keep the use of colour to a minimum (normally one or two colours will do or possibly four or five for a complex diagram). Don't go overboard with it.

Print names neatly in **CAPITAL LETTERS** directly over the area to which they refer. Use **arrows** where things may not be quite clear. Try to produce a clear overall finish, but remember — a work of art is *not* required. Don't waste time colouring everything in. You won't get any more marks, however beautiful it looks, once you have put in the basic information asked for.

Labelling

- Put labels and so on to one side of your sketch or diagram, using lines and arrows as necessary to explain things.
- Avoid lines crossing each other.
- Use both sides of the diagram for labelling if necessary. Don't draw a diagram and then write labels all over the middle of it; this will cause confusion and may cost you marks.
- Make the diagram big enough to be clear. Again a work of art is not required. In technical subjects, a simple line diagram will suffice.

The advice on labelling also applies when small diagrams are supplied for labelling — do it clearly on one side.

Example

Question 4: *Draw and label a diagram of the human upper body (showing main bones and organs).*

The first sketch (A) has all of the information needed. It is perfectly clear, and will attract full marks. The second sketch (B) has all the information, and takes the same amount of time to do as the first, but it will lose marks

Diagrams and Drawings

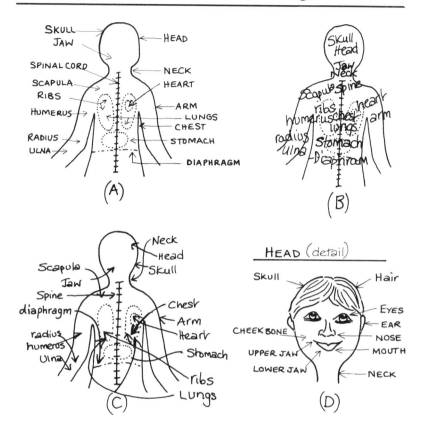

heavily as it is impossible to tell from the labelling what is supposed to be where. The third sketch (C) is clearer than the second, but it looks very messy. Marks may be lost because of the confusing crossing arrows. If more detail is required then draw larger diagrams or draw a supplementary diagram of the extra detail, as in (D).

An art exam is a different proposition, of course. The quality of the finished work is part of the overall test, and will carry a proportion of the marks. Your best efforts are required here.

You may be told *'not to write on, or otherwise mark'* a diagram which is supplied. You may have to answer the question in your answer book, possibly copying out the sketch. Again, read and follow the instructions carefully.

You may be asked in a Biology or Geology exam to draw a specimen provided. Don't try to produce a photographic representation. A simple line drawing, showing the important features you want to label, is all that is required. Use colour as necessary to make things clearer.

Doing Calculations

In Maths, Engineering and similar exams, most of the answers will probably involve calculations. As this forms most of the student's subject he or she will be well used to calculations and should need no further advice.

Being accurate

However calculations often form part of questions in many other technical or scientific subjects. They should be an easy way to pick up marks, but they can be an easy way to lose them, too. You may know the formula (or be given it in the question paper), and substitute the numbers and work out the answer quickly and confidently, especially if calculators are allowed. Then, marks can be picked up easily, and valuable time saved. But if you make one small slip leading to the wrong answer, most of the marks (only given for a correct answer) will be lost. Few if any marks will be given for the *method* itself, even if this is perfect.

I have seen this happen so often. The candidate thinks he has done well and got the right answer, but the **decimal point** may be in the wrong place (e.g. 10.875 instead of 108.75). Or the student has **divided** where he should have **multiplied**, or got the initial **formula** wrong (e.g. A x B = C + D/E instead of A x B = E/C + D), and so on. I have seen simple **slips in addition**, and simple fatal **omissions** (e.g. A x B = C + D/E instead of (A x B) + X = C + D/E). When this happens the marker may feel sorry for the student for having made such a silly slip, but he cannot give any marks (or very few).

Using the right units

Another common mistake is not being careful with **units**. You must make sure you are using the *right* units in your calculation. Some **conversions** may be necessary before or after your calculation. Usually you are not expected to remember constants or other complicated numbers. These will usually be given in the question (e.g π = 3.142 or speed of light = 186,300 miles/sec or blood temperature = 98.4°F).

Make sure *before* the calculation that the numbers you are given are in the right units. For example, you may have to convert 98.4°F into 37°C before using it. Make sure *after* your calculation that you express your result **in the units required**.

If several units are possible (e.g. kcal/mole, joules, B.Th.U., ergs, electron volts, calories — are all units of energy) usually one is favoured over the others; use this wherever possible. More leeway is allowed here in marking, however, and provided your answer is correct in the units you specify you will normally get the marks. But whatever you do, don't forget to **specify the units**. An answer of 328.6 is meaningless if it should be 328.6 yards or 328.6 mph. Omitting the units may cost you crucial marks even if the numerical answer is correct.

Be sure, and be clear

Unless you are very sure about the calculation, or it is a very easy one, forming a small part of the question, calculations are best left alone. Choose other questions, all things being equal. Of course, you may have no choice. If so, make it crystal clear to the marker what you are doing. Write down the formula you are using:

$$A \times B = (C + D)/E$$

and substitute the numbers

$$2 \times 17.4 = (27.8 + D)/3.$$

Further lines of working may or may not be necessary:

$$D = (2 \times 17.4) \times 3 - 27.8$$

Finally, work out the answer, underline it, and put in the units.

Ans. D = 76.6 gallons.

This makes it quite clear to the marker **what** your final answer is, **how** you have arrived at it, and **where** you may have gone wrong. You have not simply dreamed up a number out of thin air or made an educated guess.

Advanced calculations

In some Maths and related exams many of the marks may indeed be assigned to the method in more complex calculations. Thus marks can be gained here even if the final answer is wrong, and it is correspondingly more important to show the working method clearly.

For some subjects, an oral examination may have to be taken by everyone sitting that subject. This is usually the case with **language exams** (e.g. French) and some other subjects. In this case the oral exam will form part of your exam timetable.

Treat an oral exam as a written paper for study purposes, and for making out your revision timetable. In most cases the study you need to do will be the same as for a written paper. In an oral exam you simply **speak the answer**, rather than write it down. (In a related type of exam, the **aural** (listening) exam, you may be required to listen to the question or other material (e.g. music) and **write down** the answer.)

With languages, get as much practice as possible beforehand either with someone who is fluent, or in a language laboratory using tapes if available, or by yourself out loud. Use a tape recorder if you can to record and play back your efforts. This will help you to improve both technique and accent. Don't practise with someone who is no better than you are — it *won't* improve your ability, and may even lead to bad technique, accent, vocabulary and grammatical errors.

"Est-ce que vous avez être examinateurs oralistes depuis longtemps?"

Ad hoc orals

In some cases, an oral examination may only be required of *some* students taking the paper. This is not some kind of punishment meted out to the luckless few. Rather, it is an attempt by the examiners to be as fair as possible to everyone concerned. This may arise after marking, when a student's marks fall exactly on the dividing line between pass and failure, or between a lower and higher grade.

Borderline cases

Where the actual grade is not of vital importance, only those students on the actual borderline between pass and fail may be called for an oral. For example, with a pass mark of 40% those students having perhaps 38-42% may be called. Sometimes previous work or results may help this decision, but in most public examinations these will not be known.

In other cases the actual **grade** awarded may be vital, e.g. for university entrance requirements. In such cases those students who are on the various dividing lines between grades may also be called. For example, for A/B at 75%, B/C at 65%, C/D at 55%, D/E at 45% and E/fail at 40%, students having marks of say 74 or 66 or 55 may be considered and called. But not every such student will be called. The examiners will usually

- study the student's paper(s) again
- recheck the marks, and
- even reassess the whole paper

in order to decide for example,

(a) whether a 66 is a genuine grade B, or just lucky, so that the student should be more realistically awarded a C;
(b) whether a 74 is really a B and reflects the student's ability accurately, or whether the student who has got 74% correct really deserves another mark and should be awarded an A;
(c) whether a student having a 55 is really a C or a D.

Students are rarely marked down. Normally the benefit of the doubt is given (where it exists) and the higher grade is awarded. Every effort is made to be fair to the individual student and the whole body of students in that year and in previous years. However, as orals are time-consuming it is not feasible to interview everyone; only a minimum of borderline students will normally be called for an oral examination.

Being given a second chance

If you are called, therefore, do not be too nervous about it. Approach the oral with a **positive attitude**. After all, you have been given a second chance to pass or to better your grade (and get that vital B for university entrance).

If you are called for an oral you will be given plenty of notice. You will usually have several days to re-study and concentrate on that particular subject and be better prepared to do well. Use this time wisely; *few people get such a second chance!*

In many science or technical subjects (e.g. Biology, Chemistry, Geology) you may have to take a practical examination. In very practical subjects (e.g. woodwork, metalwork) the practical exam may form most or all the examination in that subject.

It is hard to prepare for a practical examination. A rat dissection is not easy at home, nor will your family appreciate you stinking out the house with your chemistry set. It's difficult to find diamonds or gold-bearing rocks in the back garden, and you probably won't have a band saw or lathe in the garage. But try to prepare as much as you can.

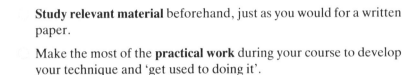

Study relevant material beforehand, just as you would for a written paper.

Make the most of the **practical work** during your course to develop your technique and 'get used to doing it'.

Try to get **extra practice** at school or college if you can.

Discuss any particular problems with your instructor.

Treat the practical **as you would any other exam** as far as possible.

● **Prepare** yourself (the night before, and on the day) taking with you whatever equipment you may need.

In the exam operate the same system of **timing and marks** for the various things you have to do in separate questions.

Again, **read the instructions and questions** carefully; comply with them to the letter. This is even more important where only your end-product is produced for assessment; the marker has no idea of how you did it or where you went wrong.

Remember you will be given everything you need to answer the question or do the task set. If you feel you need something else, by all means ask. But think about the situation first; see if by tackling it in a different way (usually an easier way) you can complete the task with what you are provided. This is almost always the case. Don't read extra difficulty into a situation where it doesn't exist.

Remember, too, that although you will be given everything needed to complete the task you may not have to use everything you are given. I remember a Physics GCE O-level practical exam where a rag provided for mopping up accidental spillages was used in all kinds of odd ways by students anxious to use everything provided.

Work smoothly, cleanly and tidily, but don't let this rob you of valuable time. Go as quickly as you can, but don't rush — this will only lead to bad work or accidents. Try to give the marker as much information about what you have done (on a piece of paper if possible). If you have a disaster make it clear what, why and where it happened. For example, 'Note — I had an accident and dropped the flask.' Or, 'In the second stage of the process the reaction failed to happen so I could not proceed further', and so on. This will help the marker sort out what has happened, and will give you some marks. If you have time at the end repeat any work you are not satisfied with if you can. Don't spend time trying to get one thing to work repeatedly at the expense of the rest of the exam. Leave it and go on. Come back to it later, only if you have time. At the end of the exam check through everything you have done as usual.

"At least the litmus paper turned blue!"

Marked examinations are of two types which will affect how the exam is to be tackled — class examinations and public examinations.

Class examinations

Firstly there is the class examination. In this, the examination is set and marked by the instructor. This is usually easier to tackle than the public examination:

- you will normally be examined only on that material covered recently in class — not on the whole syllabus or material studied some time ago.
- you have the advantage that the instructor knows you personally, and how much you know. He can probably even read your hand-writing.

It may be easier to gain marks if your instructor 'knows what you mean' when you have not expressed yourself clearly, or if he/she can decipher your handwriting enough to give you the marks. Remember, no-one is trying to 'do you down'. **Everyone wants you to pass and do well.** They will help you as much as possible to that end, but it is up to you to let them help you by proper preparation and study.

Public examinations

The second type is the public examination, and an explanation of the overall process in general may be helpful here. In a public examination (be it a school leaving certificate or university degree exam) the questions on the question paper will usually be set by *different people* who specialise in a particular area and who will be marking that particular question (where the numbers of the students are manageable).

This may help you, for instance in a university degree exam, if you know which question will be set by which lecturer. You may be aware of that particular lecturer's point of view, interest or emphasis, and you can use this to full advantage. In this case you should probably frame your answer to reflect that point of view. You may have your own point of view or theory which you privately feel is better, but unless you are specially asked for it this will not normally get you more marks.

Boards of Examiners

In other cases the questions are set by several people quite unknown to you. These questions are put together to form a question paper which will be considered by the Board of Examiners to ensure the balance is right. The paper as a whole must be fair, and the questions must represent a fair and reasonable test of the subject and syllabus, and of the standards and level of knowledge the student should have reached.

In this case you do *not* have the advantage of knowing your teacher or lecturers. The questions may be asked in a different way or format to that which you have been expecting, or are used to. This is why it is *vitally* important to read the question carefully; learn to think about what is actually being asked for before rushing into your answer. Something which at first looks alien to you could well turn out to be something you know perfectly well, but asked in a different way. You can be sure however that the examination itself is as fair as possible for all the students involved; any slight disadvantage to you is suffered equally by every other student.

External marking

When thousands of students take an examination it is not practical for one individual to mark all the papers, or even one question on all papers. In this case **external markers** are employed.

The completed scripts are normally collected at a central point. They are rechecked for names and numbers to make sure all are present and none have been lost. They will have been checked even before leaving the exam room. They are then divided into bundles of manageable numbers (usually a few hundred per bundle) and sent out to the external markers with a list of candidates' names, and a marking form. The markers will normally be teachers or lecturers qualified in the particular subject, and with plenty of experience in marking examinations.

How your script will be marked

A **marking scheme** will be provided by whoever set the question, and an overall marking scheme for the paper is thus put together. The person marking your paper, therefore, will have **strict guidelines** as to what marks must be awarded to various parts of questions and for various important points. The marker will not have much leeway to mark as he/she feels fit (some small leeway may be allowed for the discretion of the marker but instructions will normally be given as to *how* it is to be applied). This ensures a fair and even system of marking between various people (discrepancies are dealt with later).

The marker goes through each script in turn, **awarding marks according to the schemes**. If you have the answer given on the marking scheme, you will get the marks. If you do not, then you won't. The marking scheme will allow for differences of choices in answers where they occur.

The marker (who is working to a deadline) will not have time to spend hours marking your script when he/she has hundreds more to go through. This is why it is so important to make your answers clear, legible, brief, and to the point. The marker will not want to plough through pages of verbiage to see if you have one minor point or another included more by accident than intent. He/she will normally strike out long passages of rubbish or waffle. There is simply no point indulging in this practice. If you don't know the answer, then leave the question aside and get quickly on with something else.

Remember the marker is on your side. They have been through many exams themselves and know just what it is like. They hope to give you a pass or a good grade, but it is still **up to you to help them** by giving clear answers.

● You are *not* expected to produce a work of art (except possibly in an art exam).
● You will *not* be penalised for bad handwriting (except in a handwriting exam), or for bad spelling (except perhaps in an English exam).

But you may well lose marks *indirectly* if the marker simply cannot read what you have written, or if confusion arises from your bad spelling. The student will be given the benefit of the doubt wherever possible, but be clear and legible in your answer — don't scrawl it out in a rush.

Although it is usually best to answer questions in sentences, it is not required (in most cases). If time is short it is better to answer a question with a series of short phrases or part sentences which are legible, than to try and convey the same information in illegible scrawled sentences. You will probably get more marks from the first approach.

Follow the instructions

Following instructions in the exam is always vital. Suppose you were told to answer section A in one answer book and section B in another, and you answer all your questions in one answer book. The marker, who only deals with section A simply cannot mark your section B. Efforts are usually made to sort this out, and to have section B marked by the right person. But it causes great confusion, and should be avoided.

More disastrous is the case where a student is told to answer three questions from section A and three from section B — and then answers four from A and 2 from B. In this case only the three questions in section A will be marked and an entire question will be lost.

Instructions such as these are meant to ensure that students will answer questions from *both* halves of a course and cannot pass the examination on only half of a course.

It is very important here also to answer the *number* of questions asked for. Even the poorest answer will attract some marks. But do not answer *more* than are asked for. This is a dangerous practice. It is often tempting, having completed the required number of questions in plenty of time, to do an extra question or two in the hope of getting more marks. Normally this is a complete waste of time. The marker has hundreds of scripts to get through, and will not waste time marking eight or nine questions on every paper if only six had to be answered. The marker will usually mark the first six questions, and strike out the rest. Normally any time you have left after answering the right number of questions is far better spent on improving those you have already answered. Fill in gaps, check accuracy, make additional points (*see* page 77, **The Exam Itself**).

"I think that about covers it."

The end of the marking process

At the end of the marking process, therefore, the marker will have a list of names and alongside each the marks for each question attempted in their various columns and a total (and percentage) for each student. This list is then returned to the central point (along with corrected scripts) for **checking** and **tabulation** with other results.

All this process takes weeks, even months, of time and effort. This is why it can seem so long before the results are published. The more students taking the exam then the longer is the time needed for marking and checking, and further adjustment of marks. The long waiting period is not there to make students 'sweat it out'. It is needed to be **fair** to all concerned. The entire process is carried out as quickly as possible but with every care and effort to make sure no errors occur.

The pass mark for an examination, or for various grades, is usually not published. This is not because it is a secret, but because it varies from subject to subject, and even for the same subject from one year to the next. This is to make the examination as fair as possible to everyone and to help maintain consistent standards. For example, a grade given in one year must be compatible with that for previous years, and the correct proportion of pass rates must be maintained.

Examples

It is easier to explain this with examples. The pass mark is typically around 40%, but it can be higher for some subjects and quite often lower (35%) for others. Let's suppose all candidates in an exam got between 80-100 marks, or alternatively between 0-20 marks. In the former case the exam could rightly be judged as too easy — it would not be a good test of candidates' ability. In the latter case the exam was clearly much too hard for the candidates as a whole, and required a standard far higher than the students could have reached.

Adjustment of pass level

These are two extreme examples, of course, and do not happen in practice, but clearly some adjustment of the pass mark is required. All students in an exam could hardly be dismal failures, or all of them worth a distinction! Continuing with these examples, then, the pass mark may be set at 10% or 90%, and grades adjusted accordingly as an adjustment for the *standard* of the exam; a further adjustment may be needed to set the pass *rate*. If too many students in an exam fail, the marks will all be upgraded. These adjustments allow a few people to do very well, a few to fail, and most to come in between.

Raw marks

Marks are added up for each student to give a total mark for that subject. This 'raw mark' may (or may not) be out of 100. The raw mark is converted to a percentage. The 'raw percentage' marks for all students are tabulated in order. This list may be published as it is, if it is acceptable to the Examining Board.

However, no two questions can be of the same difficulty, no matter how hard the question-setters try. A situation may then occur where most questions were harder than in previous years, or vice versa. These differences may cancel out so that the paper as a *whole* is of equal difficulty to previous ones. But even so, if most of the students do the easier questions on the paper (or equally — the harder) then the result can still be distorted.

Usually the examiners will look first at the marks and their spread and the averages *from each marker* to make sure no particular marker is consistently marking higher (or lower) than the others. If this does happen (and it can), marks from that marker will be adjusted before they are tabulated into the overall list.

The examiners will then look at the overall marks, the spread, averages, pass rates, and so on, for all students and may apply a 'fudge factor' (for example multiply by 92/100 or 103/100) across the board to bring this year's results in line with previous years'. This will give a set of 'adjusted marks or percentages' to which a formal pass mark of 40% (or whatever) will be applied. From this grades will be awarded (using, for example, 75, 65, 55% as dividing lines).

No adjustment is carried out for small deviations, allowing for normal fluctuations from year to year. It is certainly true that in one year the overall level may be better or worse than in previous years, but serious discrepancies are dealt with.

Your place in the marking order

In any case the **overall position** of one student in relation to others will not be affected by this process, because it changes all marks in the same proportion. It is *this* that is important — not whether the student has 58 or 62 marks or 58 or 62%.

At this point all your hard study will be over, and it is simply a question of refreshing your memory on what you have studied for that subject. This is very necessary — it may have been weeks since you last revised the material, and you will probably have studied much on other subjects in between.

You will have finished revision two or three days before your first exam, and allowed yourself a day off, leaving one or two days for refreshing your memory on the first few exam subjects. Later exam subjects can usually be refreshed during the examination period itself.

Timetable

Make a **new timetable** based on your exam timetable, fitting in all the sessions you need for refreshing your memory. One session of three or four hours will usually be needed for each examination, although shorter periods of an hour or two will sometimes be enough (for example for practicals, where the amount of material you can study is limited). Rarely will more than one session be available before any one examination, or completely spare, but if you do find you have an extra session use it for study of a different topic, or for a rest period.

Rest periods

Normally, however, rest periods will be very few while the exams are in progress. You should be able to go for a couple of weeks without a rest period. After all, you will have plenty of time off after the exams are over to make up for it!

Planning

Try to plan the session for as soon as possible before the examination in question.

- For a morning exam this is best the night before
- for an afternoon examination the morning of the same day
- for an evening exam the afternoon of that day.

Sometimes, however, if you have a heavy timetable, with two exams on the same day, you will have to put back the revision sessions a little.

The technique of memory-refreshing

The process of refreshing your memory means working from the **revision notes** you made during earlier study and revision. It is too late now to try and work from original material — you simply won't have time to go through it all.

Read through your revision notes, in the order you wrote them out and revised them previously. This way, as you read through them again, the material will return to the front of your mind. It will help tune your brain quickly back into the subject.

Don't just *read* them, though. *Think* carefully about what you are reading, until it sticks in your mind.

- Make a few notes as you go along.
- Write out again any difficult points or parts you find hard to remember.
- After each few points have been covered try to think through them again *without* using your notes to see if you can really remember them. Write out again anything you can't.

In this way, when the exam arrives, you will actually have been through your material a total of four times (once now and three times during revision). You will have written it down, thought about it and *understood* it. You should now be completely prepared for the exam in front of you.

"You can't take them with you!"

Coping with Nerves

Virtually *everyone* taking an exam gets 'butterflies'. Indeed, a little mild apprehension can be a good thing: it can help to sharpen your concentration and focus attention on the exam. Some students, however, do get particularly worried and anxious as the exams draw near. Some effort is needed to overcome excessive anxiety, which *could* damage your chances even though you know the exam material very well. Such feelings are quite common among students taking a major public examination for the first time, and tend to decrease with more exam experience.

Correct mental attitude
The first step in overcoming the problem of pre-exam nerves is to develop a positive mental attitude. There are a number of ways of doing this.

- Convince yourself first of all that you are **studying for your own benefit** (no one else will benefit or lose if you pass or fail!)
- Try to develop a genuine **eagerness and willingness to study**. As you come to enjoy your studies more, you will find yourself actually looking forward to the exams as the culmination of your course, and the means by which you can reap the rewards of all your hard work.
- Above all, be **confident**.

Awareness
Stress is largely caused by fear of the unknown, which all of us experience to some extent. So try to make yourself *aware* of the exam and its various aspects well in advance — the marking schemes, structure of the papers and so forth. This will break down the mystique which often surrounds exams, and which causes so much unnecessary pre-exam anxiety.

Preparation
Try to become **well prepared** both physically and mentally, well in advance of the exam. Make sure you really do understand your work as you go through the course; when you come to revise you will be able to do so easily and avoid needless panic. **Be organised**; work to your own time-tables as suggested elsewhere; make sure you have everything needed for the day itself. On the night before each exam organise all the things you will need, and the right clothes to wear. All this helps you *feel* well prepared, and give an important boost to your confidence.

Other remedies
If you have done all these things, and *still* feel exam nerves building up

- try going out for a long walk
- get some good fresh air, take some deep breaths and give yourself a good talking to

- try taking some other form of vigorous exercise (swimming, cycling, playing a match, and so on) and put exams and exam nerves right out of your mind

It may help to talk to someone about the problems — parents, friends, instructors. If you do, make sure the person you talk to is someone you can really trust to be sympathetic, not someone who will only make you feel worse! Sometimes stomach pains can be caused by nerves giving symptoms of indigestion, or nausea. This can usually be cured quite easily by taking antacids such as Milk of Magnesia, Rennies and so on, from any chemist. Tension-headaches can be cured with aspirin or paracetemol. If you experience severe headaches, or migraine, stronger analgesics would be needed, and you should see your doctor if these persist.

Prescriptions

In the *last* resort a mild sedative or tranquilliser prescribed by your doctor may be useful in calming you down. I very much hesitate recommending the use of any form of drug these days for obvious reasons (risk of dependence and abuse), but there *can* be a place for this type of therapy when used properly under medical supervision.

Under *no* circumstances take any drug without consulting your doctor. You must fully explain your problem to your doctor and make it clear that you only need something to calm your nerves for the exams. You don't want anything which will leave you feeling drowsy or dopey, or affect your concentration, sharpness of wit, or slow down your thought processes.

Coping with sudden feelings of panic

If you feel nerves building up too much, or a panic attack, in the exam room:

- **stop** what you are doing
- sit up straight and **close your eyes**
- take several long slow deep **breaths**, and concentrate on staying calm and relaxing yourself completely
- concentrate your mind on **relaxing your muscles** one by one — face, neck, shoulders, arms, legs and so on.

When the problem has subsided (as it will) return to the question, and spend a couple of minutes gathering and sorting out your thoughts before starting to write again.

If you feel overcome or faint — especially in a hot stuffy exam room in the summer months — it may pay you to go out for some fresh air for a minute or two. Don't be afraid to ask — the invigilators will be sympathetic to a genuine request.

Having finished refreshing your memory, you should now be well pre-pared, and hopefully by now not suffering from any nerves. The last job before going to bed is to pack your case or bag with everything you will need for the exam. This way you won't have to rush around searching for things in the morning when you may be short of time.

Be prepared

● Take with you **plenty of everything** so you won't run out during the exam.

● Take a **spare pen** if possible. Avoid old-fashioned fountain pens and bottles of ink. Accidents can happen — spilling ink and obliterating precious answer papers. The cartridge type refill pen is best, and take a spare pack of cartridges as well. If you use biros or felt tip pens, take several of them.

● If you need to make diagrams take several **pencils**, ready shar-pened, but with a **pencil sharpener** just in case. I have known stu-dents break points off half a dozen pencils in an exam through nerves.

● A **ruler** is always useful, too.

● You may also need **coloured crayons or pencils**, **set square**, **protrac-tor**, or **drawing instruments**.

● Make sure in advance that anything you want to take with you will be **allowed in the exam**.

Calculators

Calculators are being allowed in many exams today, and are certainly very useful. Take a **spare battery** with you. Some exams however still ban the use of calculators, so make quite sure if you intend using one that it will be allowed.

A watch

One really essential item is a watch, to **time your progress**. Some exam rooms have a clock on the wall, but some do not. Have your own timepiece. Also most exams do not start exactly on time and are usually a couple of minutes late. A three-hour exam may start at 9.02 am (rather than 9.00 am) and so end at 12.02. If you are timing 30-minute questions it is better to set your watch to the hour at the start of the exam and work from that, rather than having to work to times of 9.32 and 9.47 (for half questions) and so on. If you do not own a watch yourself then borrow one. Make sure in any event that it is a good one, and not liable to stop or gain or lose time.

Make a list

Don't load yourself down, however, with a mountain of stuff you won't need. Make a careful list of what you will need, including spares, and take just that. If during the exam you find you have forgotten something, or run out of something, then put up your hand and ask the invigilators for it; they will try to get it for you. Extra items required will be provided for you in the exam, such as logtables, tables of data, graph paper, music score, materials, samples or specimens. If they are not, and you need them, do not be afraid to ask for them.

Lastly, before you go to bed, sort out your **clothes** for the following day and have them ready. Wear sensible clothes for the time of year. The aim is to be warm and comfortable in the exam room, not so 'fashionable' that you are shivering with cold or roasting in the heat.

Looking after the body

Finally, go to bed early and have a good night's sleep.

- Get up fresh in the morning, a little earlier than usual to allow for last minute problems.
- Have a good breakfast and get to the exam room promptly, well in time but not too early or nerves may build up (15 minutes before is plenty).
- Try to make sure you won't need to go to the toilet during the exam; go before if possible.
- If you are a young lady with long hair (or indeed a young man with long hair) tie it back before going into the exam to prevent the distraction of hair hanging in your face during the exam period.

Seating arrangements

Where you are taking an exam other than in your normal classroom, a **plan** of the room will usually be posted outside the exam room showing your exact **seat number or position.**

- Make a mental note of where you will be sitting in relation to the other features of the room so that you can find your place quickly and easily.
- Try to relax, be confident and stay calm. If you are well prepared, as you should be by now, you have nothing to worry about.
- Avoid silly talk with friends.

A final word

If you don't have a morning exam you will be using this time to refresh your memory for the afternoon exam. You should still have everything ready the night before, to go off to your exam after lunch. Finally it is little use taking notes to 'cram' on the bus or for the last few minutes outside the exam room. This should be unnecessary if you are well prepared. In any case the amount you will learn in such a short space of time will hardly help you now, and may only build up nerves.

Preparation checklist

Initial Preparation
- ☐ Keep a good set of notes, keep them up to date.
- ☐ Develop abbreviated style of taking notes.
- ☐ Make sure you understand material as you go along.
- ☐ Study syllabus — fill in gaps.

Revision
- ☐ Read the rules and regulations.
- ☐ Make revision timetable and stick to it.
- ☐ Study past papers, carry out analysis.
- ☐ Practise timing and marks calculations.
- ☐ Make set of revision notes as study proceeds.
- ☐ Timetable for and effectively use time off from study to relax.

Refresh memory
- ☐ Make timetable around exam timetable.
- ☐ Use revision notes made previously.

Night before
- ☐ Prepare for following day's exam(s).
- ☐ Get a good night's sleep.

On the day
- ☐ Be on time.
- ☐ Be well prepared, confident and relaxed.
- ☐ Make a note of where you will be sitting.

When you go into the exam room

- try to relax, take a few deep breaths and stay calm
- get out your pen and other things, and be ready to start.

You will have in front of you on the desk a blank answer book or paper to start with, and possibly the question paper face down. You are not permitted to look at the question paper until the official start of the exam; leave it alone until you are told to start. Sometimes the answer papers are handed out by the invigilators and you may begin immediately.

The invigilators
A word about the invigilators. They are people who are employed to ensure the smooth running of the exam. They are there mainly to help you as far as they can with any problems. Some students feel nervous because of the presence of the invigilators, who they feel are there to put them down in some way. This is *not* the case. Naturally they will see that the exam proceeds according to the rules and that no cheating takes place. But their main function is to help you as much as possible.

It may be that during the exam you will need more answer books or paper. If only one invigilator is present you can normally go up and collect your own extra paper. You may need other material (graph paper, log tables, music score) or wish to query a question or leave the room for various reasons. In such cases **do not be afraid to ask**. Simply raise your hand and wait for the invigilator to come over, and ask him/her for whatever you need.

Reading through your paper
You should have worked out in advance the **time** for each question, having allowed yourself five minutes to read the paper through.

1. Check whether the **number of questions** and **spread of marks** is as you had anticipated. If it is not, or you could not do this previously, carry out this exercise now. You should have some idea of what to expect from past papers and having had some practice at doing this during revision, it should only take a few seconds.

2. Next **read the instructions** very carefully and make sure you really understand them. Obey them throughout the exam. They will, in most cases, be as you expected, but changes do sometimes occur, so be aware of this.

3. Now **read through the whole paper**, each question in turn, but briefly and quickly, not in detail, to get a general idea of each question. In some examinations there may be questions or whole sections which do not apply to you or that you are not supposed to do. Ignore these completely — don't waste time reading them through. You could draw a line through them on the question paper to save being distracted by them later when searching for further questions.

4. **Mark off** the questions on the paper as you scan through them, writing √ or X or ? alongside them, noting which you would tackle, would not tackle, or are not sure of.

5. Now **re-examine** the questions you have ticked (√) and **pick out your best question**. Do this one first (unless instructed otherwise). Ignore any compulsory questions for the moment (unless instructed otherwise) and fit them in as you come to them (but don't forget to do them at some stage).

Answering your best question first is good for morale and good for marks. You can get down to it immediately without too much thought. It will help you to relax into a good rhythm and help you get over any initial nerves.

Starting your first (best) answer
Do read the question carefully before starting to write anything, and make quite sure you understand it. Answer

- *only* what is asked for
- *all* of what is asked for.

A note of caution here: don't start writing hell for leather just because you have spotted a familiar keyword or phrase. The question may be asking something *different* from what you first thought.

It might be worth writing a few brief **notes** or **keywords** about the question on a scrap of paper. This can be useful in essay-type answers. It helps you avoid leaving out important points. It is less useful with multiple-part answers, where it is probably just as quick to write out the actual answers direct. It is up to you.

Answer the question, then, to the best of your ability. When you have finished the question (or your allotted time for the question is up) **read the question again** to make sure you have answered all the points asked for. If you have missed anything out and have time to spare then finish it. If not, mark your question paper accordingly (mark the point(s) missed) and come back to it at the end if you still have time. **Leave a blank space** sufficient to finish the question — maybe one or two lines or half a page — before starting the next question to allow yourself room to finish it later. Above all stick rigidly to your time allowed for each question.

Your second best question

You are now ready to start the second question. Have another look at the question paper and find your next best question from those you ticked ($\sqrt{}$). Answer your second question, again reading it carefully and answering only what is required, checking at the end when you have finished or time is up. Again, if you haven't finished the question or have left out any part, **leave space** so that you can come back to it later if time permits.

Moving along

Follow instructions. In some exams some or all questions or sections have to be done in separate answer books. Feel free to pick your questions from anywhere, subject always to instructions, but be careful to answer questions in the right books and do not get these mixed up.

If you cannot finish the question within the time allowed then leave it and go on with the next one. *Remember two questions incompletely finished will usually yield more marks than one question fully finished, but which took as long to answer.* Continue with the third subsequent questions in the same way, working firstly through those questions you have ticked ($\sqrt{}$) and then progressing to the intermediate ones (?) until you have completed the required number of questions. Hopefully you will avoid all the questions you marked (X), but you may be forced to try one or more of these at the end.

Make sure that any **compulsory question** is done at some stage, even if done last and marked (X). It *must* be done even if you have a better question available. Otherwise you will certainly lose marks.

Do not attempt to answer any more questions than specified. You will not gain extra marks and you may lose marks. Usually only the *first* six (or whatever) will be marked and not the *best* six of those you have answered.

As with all rules, an exception may arise. If after completing the required number of questions you have a lot of time in hand, and spot a question that you feel you could tackle better than one previously done then by all means do this question. But *cross out* what you feel is the worst question so that it will not be marked. Make it clear to the examiner what you have done; make a note at the top or start of your paper if necessary. This should not happen if you chose the questions properly.

In some cases you may be searching for a question from among two or more apparently equal questions. In this case have regard to the type of question, and try and answer the easier one first (easier, that is, in terms of getting marks.

It may be that a choice arises between two or three alternative questions for the last or last but one question, where the situation is that you can do some of each question but not the whole of any. In this case do a quick calculation on each one to see what the maximum number of marks per question would be for the parts you can do and then do the question with the maximum potential (*see* **Timing and Marks** page 52).

Towards the end of the exam you may have to decide whether you can gain more marks from completing unfinished questions or tackling a new question which you do not have much idea about. A quick **calculation of available marks** will usually help you decide. If there is only a little unfinished material (very few marks to be gained), you could gain more marks by answering a final question — this is usually the case. If a lot remains unfinished (many marks to be gained) and you could only gain a few marks from the last question, then leave it; finish off the other questions properly first.

Completing your answers

Having now completed the required number of questions, go back and complete as much as possible of the questions you have not finished. When all questions have been answered as well as you can, go through your answers carefully and correct any mistakes or omissions.

If you have any blank spaces left in your question paper you should now draw a line through these and indicate with arrows or a note (e.g. 'P.T.O.' or 'continued next page') any continuation of answers, particularly when started on a fresh page. This will ensure that the marker does not overlook any of your answers by accident.

Finally, when you have done as much as possible or when the exam time is up, check you have your **name and number** (if applicable) on all answer papers, graph papers, drawings, and so on, and that you have filled in any other information required and that you have **complied with all other instructions**.

Time up!

Do not attempt to keep on writing when time is up. At best you will only manage a couple of lines and any further material you write down will simply not be marked. If you persist in writing on after time is called, and you have been allowed a couple of minutes grace, anything else you write will be struck out by the invigilator or a note made on your script, so there is nothing to be gained by this practice.

There is one exercise well worth doing at the end of an exam if you still have time, or as soon as you leave the exam room, and that is to make a note on your question paper (which you can normally take away) of all the answers you made. This will enable you later, when you have time, to check your answers and work out your approximate mark. This should help to boost your confidence for remaining exams, and may even help you after the results are published if your result is vastly different to the one you expected.

Last of all, forget about that exam. It's all over; you have done your best and can do no more. Good, bad or indifferent, put it behind you and concentrate on the rest ahead of you.

"I've just remembered I was supposed to get married this afternoon!"

Leaving the Exam Room

If you need to go out during an examination don't be afraid to ask. If you need to visit the toilet, feel faint, or have an unquenchable craving for a smoke, then put up your hand and ask. One of the invigilators will accompany you.

It is better to spend a few minutes to get yourself together rather than to be distracted and uncomfortable for the rest of the exam.

Try not to go out, however, unless you really need to; otherwise it is simply a waste of valuable time. You will not find the answers you seek written in the sky outside, but a few minutes' fresh air and mental relaxation may give fresh inspiration and settle nerves.

If several people want to go out at the same time you may have to wait a few minutes until an invigilator is available to go with you, and so if your problem is *really* urgent make this clear when you ask.

Having spent many hours as a marker in public examinations, ploughing through hundreds of scripts, it amazes me how many students **simply do not answer the question they are asked**. This is a widespread phenomenon. Any teacher or lecturer will tell you of the same experience.

More haste, less speed

Students in exams — under stress or in near panic with the minutes ticking away — look at a question paper and spot a question which relates to something they know about. A great feeling of relief washes over them. Off they go, writing pages of material which may be well written, full of facts, accurate and detailed. They come out of the examination room feeling good and confident and happy, and are extremely surprised when the results come out and they find they have failed the exam. The reason? — *they failed to answer the question that was asked.* They answered (often very well) a different, imaginary question and gained zero marks.

On a five or four question exam paper you would have immediately lost 20-25% of your possible marks. On a three question paper a third of your possible marks would have been lost. Also, as a perfect score is rarely achieved in any question and 15/20 can be counted as a very good mark (10/20 or 12/20 would be a reasonable average for any one question) then in terms of marks lost, and time wasted, this is **disastrous** if done once and **fatal** if repeated.

Example

For example, suppose in a literature exam you are asked to **compare and contrast** the works of poets Mr Smith and Mr Jones. Some students may have studied the works of Mr Smith in detail but never heard of Mr Jones. They proceed to write reams of excellent material on the life and work of Mr Smith. This will invariably get *zero marks* because the question is asking for similarities and differences in the style of material of Mr Smith and Mr Jones. Since Mr Jones has not been mentioned no marks have been given. The candidate quite simply failed to 'compare and contrast'.

The same could happen in a Domestic Science or Biology exam. Suppose you are asked to **discuss the nutritional value of** wheat. Students writing at length as to how and where wheat is grown and how bread is made and so on will get no marks.

The moral is very simple. It is told countless times to students by teachers and lecturers worldwide but the mistakes still go on. It cannot be stressed too strongly. It is this:

READ THE QUESTION
Then READ THE QUESTION CAREFULLY
Then THINK WHAT THE QUESTION IS ASKING FOR

Then give the answer to the question that is *actually asked*. Give a full and detailed answer to the best of your ability. Include all the points that you can think of that are relevant to the question. Do *not* write down information not asked for. It is superfluous, a waste of valuable time — *your* time — and will not gain you a single extra mark. Padding out your answer with verbiage or irrelevant facts, just to make your answer longer or more impressive-looking, will be a total waste of time. It will also probably annoy the busy marker who has to plough through this rubbish on the off-chance that you have included the right answer somewhere.

In some cases a single word or two-word answer or phrase is all that is required. In other cases a single sentence or two may be required, or a whole paragraph or several pages in an essay depending on the type of question and number of marks available.

The questions on your question paper will have been carefully checked several times before the exam. However, mistakes sometimes get through this process — such as **printing errors**. This is usually very rare in public examinations but it may be less rare in school or college exams where one person has set and produced an examination paper.

Error correction
You should therefore have some idea of how to cope with this situation. If an error is found after printing the paper but before the examination, both the error and the correction will be announced by the senior invigilator before the start of the exam. A note of the change is normally written up on the blackboard or printed on a separate piece of paper and handed out with the question paper.

If this is not the case, and you feel certain that an error exists in a question, then put up your hand until an invigilator comes over to you. Tell him/her of your problem and he/she will have the question checked out. Leave that question aside, and press on with something else until the problem is cleared up.

Guidelines
If it is impossible to have the question checked, the invigilators will probably advise you what to do. But here are some general guidelines: firstly, **avoid that question** altogether if you can. But if you *want* to do that question, or *have* to do it, then **write a note** in your answer book at the start of the question saying what you feel is wrong and how you intend to deal with it.

Examples
For example: Q. 6 *'I feel there is an error in the question and that the average walking pace of a human being is 4 mph and not 40 mph as given. I will use 4 mph therefore in my calculations.'* This is a glaringly obvious example and is probably a printing error. You would be quite safe in such a situation to proceed with what you feel or know to be right.

Another example would be: Q.2 *'There is an error in the question. Body temperature is given as 98.4°C. Body temperature is 98.4°F or 37°C and I intend using the latter figure (37°C) for the purpose of the question.'* Clearly an error in units has occurred here.

A less clear case may be: Q. 6 *'The average walking pace of a human being is given in the question as 5 mph. I feel this is an error in the question and this is too high. I feel 4 mph should be the figure given. However, for the purposes of the question I will use 5 mph as given for the calculation.'*

In this case the error is not obvious. If it is debatable, in the absence of clarification from the invigilators, it is better to accept the information as given as being correct (it usually will be). But in order to cover yourself the note you have written will explain what you have done and lead to the error being corrected during the marking process.

The **marker** will have the question checked out and if there *is* an error all other markers will then be informed. Full marks will then be allowed for candidates who have used the incorrect data (5 mph), provided their answer is correct, based on the incorrect data. Or, if they have spotted the error and used the correct data (4 mph), again full marks will be allowed.

Whatever you do, do not *do nothing*. Do not press on assuming the question is correct. The mistake may never be spotted by the marker. He/she may not know what the exact question was, and be working simply from a marking sheet with a list of correct answers.

Markers are human beings and, like the rest of us, are fallible. The marking system and process is designed to spot and eliminate errors by repeated checking and re-checking. However, in rare cases mistakes do sometimes happen. In public examinations (and elsewhere) there is a procedure to deal with this after the results have been published. This appeals procedure should not be treated lightly, however. Errors occur very rarely and an appeal is a matter of last resort.

Appeals procedure

But if, having taken advice, you feel very strongly that your result is wrong, the appeals procedure is open to you. Your paper and marks can be re-checked or re-marked and assessed by a different examiner. This is not worth the trouble if, for instance, you have been given grade C when you felt you should have got grade B, or if you have failed dismally when you thought (or rather hoped) you might just scrape through. But if you are a borderline failure and genuinely feel you should have passed, or should have achieved the required grade to go to university, then it is worth considering an appeal. Examine your conscience carefully; try to remember the exam. Should you really have done better or are you fooling yourself and wasting the examiner's time?

Fees

An appeal is open to anyone, but since it is time-consuming and creates disruption, a fee is normally payable. The fee is also designed to discourage Mrs X who feels her little Jimmy should have done much better when in fact he was a hopeless case. The fee is normally returned in cases of successful appeals, but these are rare. Otherwise it is forfeited.

It may even be necessary to show **reasonable cause** before the appeal will even be heard. You must be convinced of your facts before starting. But an appeal is well worth considering in marginal cases of great importance!

Most of this book is, I hope, positive in approach. However, I give here a list of important *don'ts* which should be observed when taking exams. Some of them may have been mentioned in other parts of the book but are included again here for emphasis.

- **Don't expect to read your notes once or twice** and walk into an exam room and do well. You won't. You may be one of the few lucky ones who always do well, but even for these people there is some room for improvement, for example in weaker subjects. Be well prepared, have a clear plan of action — then you should do well.

- **Don't arrive late** at the examination. This is obviously a waste of your precious exam time. You will not be allowed to stay longer than other candidates. Lateness is a distraction to other candidates and a nuisance to the invigilators. Worse still, in some examinations you may not be allowed in at all if you are late.

- **Don't attempt to cheat**. It should hardly be necessary to say this, but any attempt at cheating is the height of folly. In my experience cheating is actually very rare in examinations; but when it happens the cheats are invariably caught, either in the examination or later on during marking of the papers and correlation of marks. The risk of being caught is simply not worth it. No method of cheating can possibly hope to produce more than a few extra marks.

  Being caught will result in your automatic failure — not only in that exam but in all of the rest of the papers you have sat in that particular session. It may result in your being barred from taking any further examinations in that session, and will probably be noted in any reference you may need for a job. All in all, aside from the moral issue, it's a heavy price to pay for the prospect of a few extra marks! Even if you fail that exam you will be able to take it again later, and with more work and experience should be able to pass with a clean record.

- **Don't talk** to people around you or distract them. Exams are normally conducted in silence. Your actions may be misconstrued as cheating.

- **Don't take in** any books, papers or other material you are not supposed to have. However innocently this may be done, again it may be construed as trying to cheat.

Don't try to bluff if you don't know the answer by writing a lot of rubbish in an attempt to gain a few marks. You won't. The examiner will recognise waffle for what it is and draw a red line straight through it.

Don't answer more questions than you are asked for in the hope of getting more marks. You won't and it could cause you to lose marks.

Don't waste time writing out the question on your answer paper (unless you are told to). The examiners are well aware of the question asked. Make sure, however, that you number the question you are answering in the margin — and make sure the number is *correct*!

Don't rush. Exams are carefully designed so that you will have time to answer each question properly. An examiner responsible for setting a 30 minute question will *not* set a question requiring an hour to answer it. If you run out of time, you have either answered at too great a length, or spent too long thinking or dreaming, or wasted time by not being properly prepared. If you rush your answers you are bound to make mistakes. Legibility and clarity will also suffer.

Don't waste time. Invest your time carefully — for marks. Invest large amounts of time only where high marks can be won. Leave out bits which need a high time input for only a few marks. You can finish these at the end if you have time.

Don't leave any ambiguous blank spaces in your answers. Go back through your paper at the end and put lines through any blank spaces. Use arrows and notes (e.g. *PTO* or *continued*) to indicate continuation, especially if turning over a new page. It has happened that later questions and sections of students' answers have been overlooked and not marked because the examiner, seeing a blank half page, thinks the student has finished.

Don't forget to write your name and exam number (if you have one) on *all* the papers you have used. Failure to do so causes endless confusion. It is all too common.

Don't try to sit an exam if you are unwell. Get a note from the doctor if required and ask to be excused the exam. Take the exam next time round. Apart from infecting everyone else you will not do yourself justice. You need your full wits about you, and your full concentration, to do well.

Exam Checklist

Before the exam
☐ Get there in good time.
☐ Sort out your seat — make sure you will be comfortable.
☐ Settle down and relax.
☐ Get out your pens and other equipment in readiness.

Starting the exam
☐ Carry out the timing-per-question exercise, if necessary.
☐ Read the instructions carefully.
☐ Read the questions briefly and mark ($\checkmark$, X, ?).
☐ Cross out any questions or sections not applicable to you.
☐ Find your best question from those ticked ($\checkmark$).
☐ Read the question carefully.
☐ Answer it, maintaining a timing system for the various parts.
☐ When you have finished or run out of time select the second best, leaving blank spaces as necessary.
☐ Continue until the right number of questions have been answered.
☐ Go back and finish anything unfinished.
☐ Check answers for errors or omissions.

Finishing the exam
☐ Check all instructions have been complied with.
☐ Cross out any remaining blank spaces.
☐ Check that your name and number are on all pieces of paper.
☐ Note your answers on the question paper now or after leaving.
☐ Forget this exam and turn your thoughts to the next one.

For students in higher education, or mature students, one hardly needs to extol the benefits of study and exams. These students are studying because they *want* to. They have probably already had experience of exams, and on the whole look forward eagerly to completing their courses and gaining their qualifications. But for younger students still at school the benefits of examinations can appear doubtful. The terror sometimes invoked by the prospect of exams can be daunting to say the least.

This section is for the parents of such students, who will probably be from 15 to 18. My aim in offering this advice is to help them through this difficult period as smoothly as possible. Firstly it is no use whatever to nag or bully a reluctant student into an examination or to study. On the contrary, it usually has the opposite effect. The student becomes ever more resentful of the subject and more afraid of the exam. The atmosphere in the home becomes far from conducive to study.

The best approach

The best approach is one of calm discussion and reasoned argument (not rows). As a parent you appreciate the benefits of doing well in education, but your son or daughter may be too young to do so. Indeed they may have no interest in education, or even be anti-the-system. Youngsters often do not look much beyond exams or leaving school. This is because they *are* young and have little experience of life. It is the parents' role to offer them the benefit of adult experience, *but in the right way*. Young people in this age group are usually more intelligent and mature than they are often given credit for. They are capable of discussing various aspects of a problem, and will normally arrive at a sensible course of action if helped and given the chance. And remember, there can often be more than one (your own) sensible course of action to choose from.

Identifying problems

Try to find out what your own son or daughter's problems are. Which subjects do they really like and do well in? Which ones do they find difficulty with? Remember, one can *like* a subject but still not do very well at it. Try to encourage them in their weaker subjects. If you are qualified or experienced in a subject yourself, you can offer to help them directly with their work — but don't do it *for* them. You may also be able to help them get extra tuition if needed. But please discuss this with your youngster's teacher in that subject.

Talking with teachers

Indeed, try to discuss any problems with the teachers in each of the subjects at various stages during the course. Don't leave this until just before the exam; it would be too late by then. I would advise a discussion early on in the course to see how your son or daughter has settled down, and whether any change of subject is possible or desirable. Again, about half-way though the course, see how they are progressing and what difficulties they may be having, and then, several months before the exams, ask how they have coped with the course, what are their chances and whether anything can be done to improve their chances.

Don't rely on what your son or daughter may tell you. They will naturally have a different view of the situation. Nor should you always rely on **school reports** at term or year end. These are usually very brief and lack real information, although they may give an indication of any underlying problem. Discuss such a report with your son or daughter and their teacher. Most schools have **open evenings** for parents where there is an opportunity for this type of discussion. But if not, or if problems arise in the meantime, make it your business to see the teacher(s) yourself. Discuss the outcome with your son or daughter. Don't ever give them the feeling you are going behind their back. It should be a three-way input — yourself, the teacher, and the student, all working together to the same goal.

Whilst most teachers are very good at their job they are not a perfect race and there may be a few who are not quite up to scratch. If you feel this is so, having discussed matters with your son or daughter, the teacher, and possibly the school Head, then extra tuition may be the answer. But the problem may simply be a clash of personality between a perfectly good teacher and your own son or daughter. Try to discover the **root cause** of any problem and take it from there.

The independent student

It is very easy to overlook a son or daughter who seems to be doing fine. Parents after all have their own lives to lead and are busy with their own problems and the rest of the family. It is easy to forget the teenager approaching exams who does *not* bring his/her problems to you. But remember, their future is at stake, and may be determined by what happens during these crucial years. You have a part to play here, and can help them to increase their chances of a better job, career and way of life.

So, are they *really* doing fine? Make it your business to find out. Give them your attention even if they don't ask for it. But don't be overpowering. Help or attention should not be forced where it is not wanted or needed. Again, sensible discussion is the key.

Practical help

There are other practical steps you can take to help. Try to make sure the student has all the **equipment**, **books**, and **materials** needed for the course. You may not have to buy everything that is needed. If finance is a problem you can often pick up these items second-hand from shops or older students who no longer need them. The schools themselves may be able to loan books or materials in case of difficulty.

Copies of most textbooks will be available for reference or withdrawal in the school library, or public library. Expensive equipment or books may be shared by a group of students where they are not required on a daily basis; parents can get together to share the cost.

Most courses will only have one **core text** and only this may have to be purchased. Other **recommended texts** are not essential purchases; they can be referred to in libraries or borrowed from friends. On some courses it is not even necessary to own a copy of the core text, provided it can be referred to in the library; most of the material may be given out during lectures or classes, and the student's own **notes** from these classes will form the real basis of study for the exam. This is why it is so essential to take and keep good notes from classes and other set work.

A place to study
Try to ensure the student has a quiet room or area in which to study. If this is simply not possible during the course, try and make a special effort when the exams draw near and revision begins in earnest. It needs to be a room or area which is comfortable and warm, as well as quiet and generally conducive to study. A desk and chair is needed (or some substitute). It needs to be a place where the student can leave out books, papers and notes, undisturbed if possible, away from the disruptive attentions of younger children and even house-proud mothers (however well-meaning).

The art of being sympathetic
In the month or two before the exams, and during them, try to bend more towards the needs of your son or daughter, even if this requires some actual disruption of your normal routine. Try especially hard to avoid rows during this stressful period. Try to keep younger children especially quiet and away from bothering the student. If a quiet study room is not available arrange a domestic timetable when the television/radio/stereo is turned off *completely* for a couple of hours. Try to be encouraging and show interest, but don't be a nuisance or overpowering! There is no need to allow them to take over the house completely. If you have difficulties at home they may be able to study at school, with friends, or in the local library.

All in all, exams can be almost as stressful a time for parents as the students, but I hope this advice suggests at least a few ways in which the family can unite in what is after all a worthwhile cause!

Exams are hard work, and rightly so, if they were not then everyone would pass, and the exam and qualification would become quite valueless. The methods and principles outlined in this book are not in themselves a guarantee of success. Furthermore they may not suit everyone equally. It's rather like teaching someone to walk — everyone does it, but everyone does it slightly differently. One person's way may not exactly suit another.

But do study the technique in this book and try it for size. See how it fits *you*. You may want to adapt or develop it for yourself. When doing revision, for example, you may prefer to study just one subject on one day over three periods, rather than three different subjects. Maybe you can only cope with two sessions a day, not three. You may prefer to lengthen the revision period a little — but don't make it too long or you may begin to forget the earlier material as the exams approach.

Being systematic

There is no one right way of doing exams (although there are many wrong ways). I offer my experience gained over many years from *both* sides of the examination desk. It is a good sound system, but it is not the *only* system. The important thing is not which system you use but that you have a system and stick to it. The systematic approach will always give better results than any hit-or-miss method. By using this technique you will be well prepared physically and mentally, be well-grounded in your subject matter, confident and happy and even quite looking forward to the exam. You will be in a relaxed frame of mind knowing what to expect, and knowing you can handle it. In this state of mind and readiness you cannot fail to do better than you would without this preparation.

I wish you every success with *your* exam!

How To . . . Books
Opening Doors of Opportunity

A major series of self-help paperbacks packed with valuable information on new opportunities in today's fast-changing world. Each of these user-friendly handbooks gives clear up-to-date information and advice, prepared by experts, and complete with checklists for action and self-assessment material. The guides will save you time and money by supplying essential information which is often hard to find.

Helpfully clear layout with illustrations and cartoons, glossary, useful sources, index. Each 215 x 135mm, £4.95 approx.

You can't afford to miss the 'How To . . . series'

How to Get That Job Joan Fletcher
A guide for job hunters of all ages.
0 7463 0326 2

How to Pass Exams Without Anxiety David Acres
A step by step guide to removing stress and achieving success in exams at every level.
0 7463 0334 3

How to Live and Work in Australia Laura Veltman
The unique handbook for all those considering employment and residence 'Down Under'.
0 7463 0331 9

How to Live and Work in America Steve Mills
Packed with new ideas on home life, leisure, travel, social and business opportunities.
0 7463 0323 8

How to Help Your Child at School John West-Burnham
Vital information and advice for every concerned parent.
0 7463 0329 7

How to Enjoy Retirement Harry Gray
Utilising a lifetime's skills and experience for a happy and productive retirement.
0 7463 0323 8

How to Claim State Benefits Martin Rathfelder
Making sense of the system.
0 7463 0505 2

Dozens more titles in preparation. For details please contact Dept BPA.

Northcote House Publishers Ltd., Harper & Row House, Estover Road, Plymouth PL6 7PZ, United Kingdom.
Tel: Plymouth (0752) 705251 Telex: 45635.

Index